MW01295646

SECRETS TO RAISING CAPITAL

SECOND EDITION

By Michael S. Manahan

Copyright © 2020 Michael S. Manahan

All rights reserved

The characters and events portrayed in this book are fictitious. Any similarity to real persons, living or dead, is coincidental and not intended by the author.

No part of this book may be reproduced, or stored in a retrieval system, or transmitted in any form or by any means, electronic, mechanical, photocopying, recording, or otherwise, without express written permission of the publisher.

ASIN: 1452849986

CONTENTS

PREFACE

I first published **Secrets to Raising Capital** in late 2011. At the time, it provided a very comprehensive set of guidelines for understanding the complex world of raising capital. However, even though the manuscript was published less than ten years ago, the capital-raising world has changed and continues to change. For that reason, I made the decision, in early 2020, to edit my original manuscript and to publish the second edition of Secrets to Raising Capital.

I wish I could report that the world of raising capital has changed for the better – that now it has become easy for early-stage companies, start-ups, and even established companies to raise money. After all, we now have crowdfunding, peer-to-peer lending platforms, angel investor groups, and family offices all looking to invest in promising deals. Unfortunately, the reality is that raising money is as difficult as it ever was, and maybe even more difficult. In the following pages, I will discuss some of the reasons why raising capital has become even more challenging.

With the stellar economic recovery we have had since the 2008 recession, combined with a renewed interest in entrepreneurship at universities and colleges, there are more businesses than ever chasing available investment capital. That means more competition for you as you work to get the capital you need. The good news is that for those founders and CEOs who are prepared to learn and to do the work others are not prepared to do, there is a lot of capital available. You can significantly increase your chances of raising that capital if you read and follow the guidelines in this book.

At the same time, as I write this Preface, government lockdowns and draconian rules and regulations in response to the COVID-19 virus have put our economy into a tailspin. Investors and lenders have reacted as many do in times of crisis – pulling in their horns and ceasing lending and investing activities until the economy once again begins to recover. *Recover it will!* And when that recovery happens, investors and lenders will once again be looking for opportunities to deploy capital. The question will be, as it has always been – who will get the money? In my opinion, it will be those businesses that are prepared for and who understand the process of raising capital.

I see this book as also adding to the body of knowledge that is out there to help businesspeople, and particularly small businesses and entrepreneurs. While the *Wall Street Journal* and *Fox Business* focus on big corporations, the reality is that most people in the United States work for small businesses. And typically, as we pull out of recessions, new jobs are mostly created by small businesses. I teach Entrepreneurial Finance at California State University Dominguez Hills. I use an academic textbook that is filled with theory and complicated formulas. That book is great for academics. But it lacks what I call the "real-world applications." I am not sure any entrepreneur picking up that textbook would have any roadmap to guide her through the capital raising process. Secrets to Raising Capital, on the other hand, is just such a guidebook. It lays out step-by-step what you need to do to get capital for your business.

My career in business began with accounting. My first real business job was with a division of Cummins Diesel, the big diesel engine manufacturing company - after delivering newspapers, working on a dude ranch, and bartending at weddings. As a junior accountant, my job was to reconcile general ledger accounts. The work suited me. For some reason, the logic of accounting appealed to my sense of order. Accounting is predictable. It's a closed system with predictable results. If revenue goes up and costs remain the same, your profits will increase. If costs go up and revenues stay the same, your profits will decrease. If you make a debit entry, you must make a credit entry equal in value. If you make a credit entry, you must make a debit entry equal in value.

Understanding accounting helped me develop a skill that every business needs—the ability to build business models that forecast future results. Of course, the accuracy of any model is dependent upon the degree to which the assumptions used in the model mirror what happens in the real world. But even when dealing with the unknowns, accounting allows a business to predict with a high degree of certainty, the outcomes assuming some event occurs or some input value is correct. So, with a good accounting model, if you predict a sales increase of say 10%, you will be able to predict other information important in managing your business, such as how much inventory you will need, how large your accounts receivable will be, how many staff-hours will you need to support the organization and how much cash you will need for your business.

An accounting system is a logical, predictable system that can be applied to virtually every business and organization in the world. It works, it is portable, it is expandable, and it can produce an almost infinite degree of analysis and information. But the logic and symmetry of accounting fooled me. Having accounting as my first real introduction to the world of business, it came as a shock when I discovered that much of what goes on in business almost defies logic and is entirely unpredictable. I somehow thought of business with the recipe predictability of a baker. A known quantity of flour, sugar, butter, milk, and flavorings, mixed in a certain way, and cooked at a certain temperature, will time and again produce a cake of the same size, taste, color, and texture. In business, however, you can take the same number of people, with the same education or training, the same budget, the same work environment, and the same products and get amazingly different results. That same unpredictability applies equally to raising money.

You will see as you read this book, I have time and again been left scratching my head wondering why a deal I thought was stellar couldn't seem to raise money. In contrast, another deal I thought was ridiculous had raised a ton of money. I'd like to think it was my inability to pick losers and winners. However, over the years, so many of those deals I thought were dogs actually turned out to be dogs, that it convinced me there were other forces at work, which unlike my logical accounting, didn't seem to make much sense on the surface.

As I spent time talking with local bankers, investment bankers in New York, venture capitalists in Silicon Valley, high net worth individuals, factors, and hard money lenders, I came to understand that my logical model of business based on my foundation in accounting simply didn't apply. A client of mine writes books on the psychology of dating. When comparing his thoughts and ideas on how men and women interact during the dating process to how "money guys" act when looking at deals, I came to a truly startling conclusion. You can throw the logic of business out the window. Investing money and lending money, once you get past a few basic rules, is an emotional roller coaster of personalities, egos, trends, beliefs, and relationships. What does that mean to you, the person looking for money for your business? It means the more you understand how the psychology of money guys works, the greater likelihood you will have of getting the money you need.

Once I understood there was more to getting money than

a crisp business plan and a comprehensive set of projections, I started to search for information on how the money guys really work. What did I find? Dozens, if not hundreds of books were telling me to write a great business plan, develop a great strategy, and create some fabulous projections. A few books provided glossaries or descriptions of different terms, such as the difference between an investment banker and a private equity investor. Some books even included links to websites or other lists of banks, lenders, investment bankers, funds, and other money sources. But I could not find one book that explained how to deal with the psychological aspects of raising capital. What really goes on in the mind of a money guy when he or she is reading your business plan, reviewing your numbers, listening to your presentation, and considering putting up the money you need for your business? A lot is going on, and if you don't understand it, your chances of getting the funding become just that much more difficult.

That's why I decided to write this book. I like to think of it as a dose of reality and practicality. It's a real-world guide to help you navigate the tricky waters of raising capital and dealing with the sharks and alligators swimming in those waters. It explains the psychology behind the guys with the money—why they ask the questions they do, why they act the way they do, what motivates them, and how you can increase your chances of getting their attention and their money.

I hope you enjoy reading this book, as much as I've enjoyed writing it. I also hope you will glean from its pages information and ideas that will help you get the money you're looking for.

Michael Manahan
Long Beach, California
July 2020

MICHAEL S. MANAHAN

INTRODUCTION

Obtaining funding for your company—public or private; early-stage, turnaround, or growth; debt or equity—is a tough job. It's not only a tough job; it is costly in terms of both time and money. I frequently run into business people from companies (large and small) that underestimate the cost, time, and energy involved in raising capital, and further, who don't understand the process well enough, and as a consequence, make significant mistakes that cost even more time and money.

Think raising money is easy? If it were easy, those Wall Street investment bankers wouldn't be able to charge the huge fees they do for raising capital. Wall Street money guys make tens and even hundreds of millions of dollars raising money, and even then, they often don't succeed. Read the *Wall Street Journal*, and you will read of money-raising failures—IPOs that have been pulled from the market, syndicates falling apart, businesses forced into bankruptcy due to a capital squeeze. If you ever read an investment-banking contract, you'll see that investment bankers often only promise a "best efforts" basis. What does that mean? It means they get paid, even if they don't bring home the bacon!

So, what does that mean to you? If the Wall Street guys sometimes don't raise money, does that mean your chances are next to zero? No, not at all. But if you are trying to raise money for a company you own or you work for, regardless of its stage or its size, you will greatly increase your chance of success by knowing the *Secrets to Raising Capital*. Are there really secrets to raising capital? Yes!! There are secrets because most people don't know those, and the few who do, won't tell you.

Who am I to be telling you how to raise money? And why should you listen to me? Let me explain it to you. My education and formal training are primarily in finance and business. I grew up in Vancouver, Canada, and became a Chartered Professional Accountant. That is a Canadian equivalent of a Certified Public Accountant. After moving to Southern California over thirty years ago, I earned my Master of Business Administration from Pepperdine University. I am also a full-time lecturer in finance and accounting at California State University Dominguez Hills. On top of that, I am a business owner, real estate investor, and consultant.

With that background, I have spent the better part of my thirty-plus-year career helping companies raise money. I have raised both equity and debt from traditional banks, hard money lenders, lessors, factors, angel investors, private equity funds, hedge funds, family offices, and through IPOs. And I have done this fund-raising both as an employee of the company trying to raise capital (Chief Financial Officer or President) and as an advisor and consultant to the company raising the capital. I am not a Wall Street Guru, I never worked for Goldman Sachs or Morgan Stanley, and I don't profess to be a Michael Milliken protégé. But I have worked with well over one hundred management teams in my career, from start-ups to billion-dollar corporations. Most of my work at one point in time or another had me involved in the process of raising capital. In that process, I've succeeded, and I have also failed. In some of those instances, the results were well beyond my control. But to the degree I did have control, I can tell you I obtained funding for the companies I represented by putting some basic principles to work—principles not known by most people looking for money.

Ask any MBA grad how to raise capital, and you'll get a pretty standard response (go ahead; try it—I have, and it's amazing what MBAs don't know about raising money). First, you need a good plan. Second, you need a nice set of financial projections. Third, your plan and your projections should support a great strategy. With these documents in hand, venture out into the world of angel investors, venture capitalists, investment bankers, fund managers, private equity groups, traditional business banks, leasing companies, factors, hard money lenders and anyone else you can find to present your plan to, and you'll get the money.

Well, maybe you will, and maybe you won't (we'll talk more about business plans a little later). But suffice it to say that even with a good business plan and a great strategy, getting funded is just not that easy. In addition to the business plan, you need a lot more arrows in your quiver to get the attention of the people with the bucks. And that's where the *Secrets to Raising Capital* comes in. In these chapters, I'll teach you how to put your company at the top of the list, how to shine in front of the money boys, how to make your deal stand out amongst the other deals on the desk, and how to substantially increase the chances of getting funding for your company.

Remember something about money-guys. You may think it is their job to invest or lend money. It's their job **not** to invest or lend money. That's because they spend more of their time figuring out <u>why</u> not put their money to work than figuring out <u>how</u> to put their money to work. That means, most deals that cross the desk of any money guy get rejected (Don't believe me? Just ask one). Money guys search your documents, your background, your industry, and maybe even your factory floor looking for a reason to put you and your deal on the reject pile.

MICHAEL S. MANAHAN

It's not only about convincing the money guys that your deal is worthy of their money, but it's also about convincing the money guys that your deal is better than the other deals they have sitting on their desk (which in some cases could be dozens of other deals). No money guy has the time to look at all the deals that come his way. So, what does he do? He looks for reasons to reject the deal, to take the deal and throw it on top of the pile of deals he has on the shelf in his office, or his credenza.

What does this mean to you? It means that your deal is not being looked at in isolation. Your deal is being weighed against all the other opportunities the money guy has in front of him. Because he doesn't have the time to look at every deal, he is focused on identifying reasons to reject most of the deals on his desk. Your job is to reduce the number of reject points. Once you're at the top of the heap, then you'll have a chance of the money guy taking a serious look at you. By following the ideas, guidelines, rules, and suggestions in this book, you will significantly increase your chances of not being rejected and of getting the funding you need for your business.

I need to mention two additional issues. First, this book is equally applicable to companies looking for debt and companies looking for equity. Most of the strategies and tactics outlined herein apply equally to both. For convenience sake, and so as not to be repetitive, I may use lender in one spot and investor in another, but remember that there are many gradients on the scale between pure debt and pure equity, and most of the concepts, we will be discussing, apply to money raising in general, whether you are trying to raise debt, equity, or some combination of both.

Second, this book is not just for start-ups or mom-and-pop businesses. While I think this book will be of extreme value to small companies and fledgling enterprises, I could fill another book about what the executives at some larger cor-

10

SECRETS TO RAISING CAPITAL

porations don't know about raising capital, and I give some examples of that in this book. That's not to say the executives are not qualified for their jobs. But remember, a CEO's job entails many day-to-day activities revolving around production, sales, human resources, and effective enterprise management. With a few exceptions, even in larger companies, the CEO does not spend most of his or her time on the warpath looking for capital. Some of these CEOs have investment bankers to do the work for them, but many investment bankers (or at least people who call themselves investment bankers, which could be someone working out of his garage) don't know what they are doing either. Having worked in large enterprises and as a consultant to large enterprises, I have concluded that the material in this book would be of tremendous benefit even to large company executives who are open to learning and doing their jobs better. Although from experience, I have learned that the learning capacity of many of the CEOs in this country is very low, and that may explain why they make so many stupid mistakes.

When it comes to raising capital, there are three groups of people who are successful. The first group includes people who just got lucky—maybe they had a rich relative, were in the right place at the right time, won the lotto, or happened to find a stupid investor or lender. I know one business owner who financed his business from the settlement he received in a medical lawsuit. It happens, and if you are lucky enough to be this person, you probably wouldn't be reading this book. The second group of successful money raisers is the Slick Willies. These are the guys who can schmooze and charm the pants off anyone. I've seen some of these guys in action, and believe me, they are impressive. I met a doctor who had convinced a group of venture funds to put up $80 million into a medical technology that, in my opinion and the opinion of many of my colleagues, was about the craziest idea on the planet. But this doctor could hold an audience and schmoozed the money right out of the bank accounts of these venture capitalists. I am going to presume you're not a Slick Willy, because if you were, you wouldn't be reading this book. By the way, from experience, the lucky ones, and the Slick Willies probably account for about 1 percent of the money raised by corporations (my estimate).

So, who is the third type? They are those business people who work smart, learn something about the capital raising process, get their deal in front of money guys with the interest and capacity to fund the deal, and finally, make their deal look better than the other alternative uses of the money guy's funds.

As a final word in this introduction, this book is <u>NOT</u> a list of money guys. It's not a reference book of funding sources. You won't find the contact information of a venture capitalist, investment bank, lender, or any other capital source in this text. Why? Finding funding sources is easy. All you need to do is run a few Google searches on the Internet. There are thousands of them. Getting them to fund your deal is hard. Really hard! But with the information in this book at your fingertips, when you do find those funding sources, you'll have the strategies, ideas, and information you need to get the money!

THE RECIPE FOR RAISING MONEY

Before getting into the secrets of raising capital, I want to spend some time discussing the actual process, or recipe, for raising capital. I use the word recipe because, to me, effective money-raising is just like cooking. Certain ingredients are needed, certain steps must be taken, and there is an order in which those steps should be taken, and those ingredients used, to get the end result. Also, raising money is kind of like cooking because it's not just about the food; it's also about the presentation. If you've ever watched the television show *Iron Chef*, you have seen that the competing chefs get points not only for taste but for what they call plating. Plating is how the food is presented. I like the *Iron Chef* analogy for another reason. Typically, the food prepared by both chefs is cooking at its finest. Most of us would be lucky to be able to eat food so well prepared. Yet, even though two sets of fabulous meals are presented to the judges, only one chef walks away the winner.

Raising money is also a competition. You are competing with every other business that is out there looking for capital. And no matter how good your business is, only so many businesses will get funded. As in the *Iron Chef* Television show where you get points for presentation, in the money-raising arena, you also get points for presentation. In fact, how your company is perceived by the money guys is as important in getting funding, as is the business itself. Why? Because the packaging is as important as the product, and to get the financing your business needs, you need to package your business properly.

Packaging your business properly is part of the recipe for raising capital. But what exactly is the packaging of a business? The packaging is everything the money guys see and hear about your business when making the decision to give you the money. Your employees and your customers probably know your business well. They know your business from personal experience—from using your products, delivering your products, or making your products. But a money guy doesn't have that first-hand experience. He gets his impression of the merits of your business from what he sees and hears, and most of what he sees and hears come from you. Therefore, in order to make the best impression possible, you need to package your business properly, and that's why, in the recipe for raising capital, there are a lot of steps involved in packaging prior to getting funding. Keep this in mind as you read the rest of this book.

So, what are the steps in raising capital? They are as follows:

- Preparing a business plan (Word. PowerPoint, or both)
- Preparing financial projections
- Preparing a two-page summary of your business *one!*
- Preparing a five-minute pitch ✔
- Preparing a PowerPoint presentation (pitch deck)
- Preparing a speech to go along with your presentation (pitch) ✔
- Practicing your speech and your pitch
- Identifying funding sources
- Contacting funding sources
- Pitching your deal to funding sources
- Making formal presentations to funding sources

- Obtaining term sheets
- Completing the due diligence process
- Completing final documents
- Getting the money

Through the remainder of this book, I will take you through these steps and identify for you the areas where you can make your company (and you) look better than the competition, how to avoid situations and circumstances that could reduce your chances of getting funded, and give you secrets on what to say and how to act that will substantially increase the chances of you getting the capital you want and need.

BUSINESS PLANS AGAIN

OK, I'm starting off with business plans—you already know that you need a business plan. Remember, that's what all our MBA grads said we would need to help us raise money. Or they used to say it. There are voices suggesting that business plans are no longer necessary.

Recently the head of one of those university incubators for start-ups said to me, "We stopped using business plans ten years ago!" So, what do they use instead? Something he calls a skinny business plan. What is a "skinny business plan?" A business plan that is shorter than long business plans, and a business plan that "gets to the point." Well, I was never a big fan of those 50-page business plans, in part, because many of them were full of unimportant and inconsequential information.

Further, because the plan was so long, the authors didn't think they needed to include the information that investors really need and want to know. It was sort of the attitude, "Well, if 50 pages don't tell you what our business is all about, what else could you possibly want?" Even if it's a "skinny business plan," you still need a business plan.

A few years ago, a Syracuse University professor, Carl

Schramm, published a book titled *Burn the Business Plan*. Schramm suggests that rather than a business plan, an entrepreneur needs "innovative ideas, real-world experience, and keen judgment." I think the title was more of a marketing gimmick than actual condemnation of planning. At some point, you must take your ideas, your experience, and your judgment and decide what to do, and why wouldn't you write down what you've decided to do, once you decide? A 2018 article in Forbes was titled, *Don't Waste Time on a Startup Business Plan -- Do These 5 Things Instead.* The five things include developing a pitch deck that would consist of: Company Overview, Mission/Vision of the Company, The Team, The Problem, The Solution, The Market Opportunity, The Product, The Customers, The Technology and a few more items. Well, that certainly sounds like what you would put in a business plan to me.

What happens when I tell people who are trying to raise money that they need a business plan? For those who don't have a business plan, I typically get two responses. The early-stage companies and entrepreneurs like to refer to some story they read in a book about some guy who raised $50 million by writing his business plan on the back of a cocktail napkin in some midtown Manhattan bar while drinking $14 martinis (the ones that now cost $25). Maybe that happened. But for that one guy who funded his business on a cocktail napkin, the thousands of other businesses that got funded had a business plan. If you want to get funded, I suggest you have a business plan too.

The other response I get, typically from mature companies that maybe haven't had to look too hard for money in the past is, "All our last banker wanted to see was our financial statements. We've been in business for twenty years. We've been making the best propane barbeques in the state for all that time; our customers include Costco and Walmart, and the governor has one of our barbeques on his back patio." All of that may be true, but most of the companies that got funding from that bank you're talking to got funding, in part, by providing a business plan, and I suggest you do the same. It may be easier to write those business plans if you've been in business for 20 years, but you still need it.

I am not going to tell you how to write a business plan. There are plenty of resources out there that will do a great job of guiding you through the process. There are books, software packages, and even consultants who will help you put your plan together (do a Google search for software and consultants or do a search on Amazon.com for books). Even better, you can hire me!! But what I am going to tell you is how you need to write your business plan to make it more effective. The following are some of the key elements you need to pay attention to for your business plan to get the most attention.

Spelling and grammar. Yes, it does matter. Assuming a potential funding source takes the time to read your plan (and if they get serious, someone from their team will), they will judge the plan as a reflection of the quality you put into the execution of your business. A sloppy plan can give the impression that you run a sloppy business. Word processors have spell and grammar checks—use them. If your English isn't that good, have someone who has a better grasp of the language check it over for you. We live in a country of immigrants, and I have seen business plans written by people who could barely speak English. Some of those were terrible —a torture to read. Some were great. If putting something on paper is not one of your greatest skills, get someone else to check it. (And by the way, to be a CEO, writing doesn't have to be one of your best skills; I've worked with CEOs of companies worth billions of dollars who could not send an email without it containing a dozen spelling and grammatical errors). If you don't know someone, or you don't have a staff member or colleague capable, you can probably find a professional writer on Upwork or Fiverr or some other gig website that will do it for a small fee. Regardless of content, poor grammar and spelling errors will reflect poorly on you and may even be a negative consideration in the funding decision.

Consistency. Consistency in your business plan is extremely important. In fact, it is essential not just in your business plan, but in your presentation, your fact sheet, and even in what you say when you talk to funding sources about your company. We'll talk more about presentations and fact sheets later, but let me explain what I mean about consistency. **Inconsistency relates to statements or assertions in your plan that may *conflict* with other statements or assertions in your business plan.** When reading your plan, the reader probably doesn't know if a lot of what you put in your plan is true, and in fact, the reader understands that a lot of what you have in your plan cannot be proven. A business plan includes estimates, forecasts, guesswork, assumptions, and claims. Money guys understand that, and you can include some very aggressive assumptions and claims in a business plan. It's not your job to be conservative in your plan, but it is your job to be consistent.

Let's take an example to illustrate inconsistency. Frank's Surfboard Company has been in business for ten years and is now profitable, doing $10 million a year. So, Frank goes to his local banker (the one that still makes business loans – there are not that many left) and applies for an expansion loan. Frank wants to borrow $2 million to finance working capital and an expansion of his production facility. In his business plan, Frank claims that one of the reasons for his success to date is his ability to appeal directly to what today's surfers are looking for. Frank has a team of surfers who hang out at all the surf beaches, who feed him information on trends; he adapts those trends into his design, and this has made him a leading manufacturer in Southern California. This is an assertion that is very difficult to prove or disprove. It's possible; it's also plausible, and, if correct, certainly explains Frank's success. In fact, it demonstrates that Frank understands what drives his business, and is on top of satisfying customer demands and changing market conditions.

Frank also includes in his business plan a discussion of his sales strategy. He has five sales guys who travel from surf shop to surf shop. Frank says in his business plan that the decision on which surfboard to buy is really influenced by the guys who work in the surf shops, and what they recommend, the surfers will buy. So, his sales guys spend a lot of time making friends with the guys who work in surf shops, giving them jackets, t-shirts, and baseball caps, buying them beer, and hanging out with them at various events. This is the reason for their strong sales growth. Again, this is an assertion that is difficult to prove or disprove. It's possible, and it's plausible. And it shows Frank has a good understanding of what drives the market and the key role the surf shops play in driving sales.

However, while both of Frank's assertions may be true, they conflict with one another. Either it is the design of the boards in tune with what surfers are looking for, or it is the relationship with the guys in the stores who recommend Frank's boards, that drive his sales. Either, surfers buy based on performance and features, or they buy based on the recommendation of surf shop employees. To attribute sales success to both is an inconsistency. It is the type of inconsistency that would have the reader concluding not that Frank is a savvy businessman who knows his market, but that Frank really doesn't understand what is driving his sales.

When I have seen money sources identify these types of

inconsistencies in a business plan, the typical response from the businessperson has been, "Well, they are both important. If the customer doesn't buy because of our product design, then he buys because the guy in the surf shop recommends the product." While that may be true, it doesn't explain what still appears to be an inconsistency. The reader of your business plan is looking for the differentiators—the actions you are taking, the features you have, the way you do what you do, that puts you ahead of the competition—what gives you a competitive edge. Is your competitive edge your understanding of the surfer mentality? Or is it your close relationship with the boys in the surf shops? You better figure out which one it is and focus on that one success factor as being your major competitive advantage.

Understanding the distribution system. Another big failure in business plans is in understanding the distribution system of the industry in which the company operates (by distribution system, I mean how the product/service gets from the business to the customer, including the buyer decision-making process). This problem is probably more related to newer enterprises but also relates to more mature companies that are looking to expand their markets.

I'll give you a couple of examples. One I have seen repeated over and over again is a company that is launching a new product, or just trying to expand its market, and is going to drive sales by selling to big-box retailers (that means companies like Walmart, Target, Costco, and The Home Depot). The company has never sold to anyone of these retailers in the past yet is going to go out in year one and sell millions of dollars to these companies. It could happen, and it probably has, but to anyone who understands how the buyers in these big retailers work, such forecasts are extremely unrealistic and inconsistent with reality. Buyers at big retailers are hesitant to make big product launches. They don't know if you can ship on time, if your products work properly, or if you have the financial resources to handle a big order. So, most likely, you would get a trial order, and your product would be introduced in a small number of stores. Then, based on sales and your ability to deliver and the product to sell through, the orders would be increased over time. It could take years to get the order volumes you want, and if your products don't sell through, then no further orders may be forthcoming unless you are able to drive product demand through marketing.

A similar lack of understanding of the distribution system appears in a lot of business plans when the product is something that will be purchased by some form of government institution (federal, state, or municipal government; post office, military, etc.). These institutions are characterized by extremely bureaucratic purchasing processes that may be very lengthy, involve many convoluted steps like bids, RFPs, and trials, and it may be politically motivated. A fast ramp-up in sales is unlikely to occur in these industries, so business plans that include fast ramp-ups of sales, or fast selling cycles, will be inconsistent with the way those markets operate.

Making incorrect assumptions about how the distribution systems work in your business plan is one of the fastest ways to have your plan tossed on the garbage heap. If you don't intimately know how the distribution system of the industry in which you plan to operate works, then find an expert who does and incorporates everything he or she says into your plan. In fact, describe in your plan how the distribution system does work, and you will get a lot of extra points from the money guys.

<u>Tie the numbers.</u> If you are not familiar with the term, *"tie the numbers"* just means <u>making sure the numbers agree</u>. For a business plan accompanied by a set of financial projec-

tions, it is important that all the numbers in both the written part of the plan and in the projections agree. Now, I can just hear the CFO of some publicly-traded company reading this and saying to herself, "How stupid. This stuff is so obvious an idiot knows that." My response to that comment is that I was reading the business plan of a publicly-traded company, written by the CEO (MBA and engineer) and the CFO (MBA and CPA), and in the business plan, it made two statements. First, it said they planned on generating $1 million in sales from a product launch in foreign markets. But when I looked at their projections, there were no sales from foreign markets. Second, in the business plan, it said they needed $10 million to finance inventory and receivables. In fact, in their projections, only about $3 million was used for inventory and receivables. Finally, their projections also only included $5 million in funding, when the body of their business plan stated they needed $10 million.

These are the kinds of mistakes that are easily caught, but if not caught, go a long way to tarnish the image of the company and the management team. It's one of the best ways to lose credibility with the money guys. Make sure you check and double-check all the interrelated financial assumptions in your plan. If you say you need five salespeople, and you expect each salesperson to generate $50,000 a month in sales, then your sales projection is $250,000 a month. If you project $300,000 per month, someone is going to pick up the error. If your factory capacity is 10,000 units a month, and you sell your product for $10, your maximum monthly revenue is $100,000, so if you project sales of $150,000 per month, your plan better include an expansion of your facility. I know all of this seems obvious, but I stress again that I have read dozens of business plans prepared by seasoned executives with graduate degrees who miss these simple mistakes. So, tie in all the numbers. Check them and double-check them.

<u>How do you get your product to market?</u> In terms of business plan errors, glossing over this information is perhaps the biggest one. I have seen it over and over and over again, and if your plan is written this way, you might as well give up looking for money. In fact, I reviewed a business plan not long ago for a technology-related product that neglected to detail this issue fully. The business plan was about sixty pages. Of that plan, about fifty-five pages were dedicated to the product and the technology behind the product. Two pages were dedicated to how the company was going to get the product to market.

You need to include some technical information on your product, and I use the word "technical" very loosely. That means if your product has a Zinc Chrome plating to keep it from rusting, you don't need to give us the molecular structure of the plating, nor do you need to spend five pages describing how you apply it. The technical part of your product description (I use the word product to include services as well, as there is a technical component on how services are delivered) is a brief summary of its features, design, product, or utilization, and how each of those items you have mentioned translates into product superiority or cost advantage.

As an example: "Through our patented interlocking collapsible design we can package our finished product in a shoe sized box, while our closest competitor's product comes in a box the size of a 26" television, meaning our shipping costs will be two thirds less than our major competitor, giving us a substantial cost advantage, particularly in markets farthest from our factory, and for mail order shipments."

You don't need to include the facts that it took your mad scientists three years to come up with the design, that you went through fifty-two iterations before you got it right, copies of six schematic diagrams of how the design works, test results, bar charts, copies of patents, and a host of other superfluous information that is not germane to the issue. In fact, if you provide too much information, you lose the reader. He or she may miss the point you are trying to make—that your design gives you a substantial edge over the competition in the marketplace.

I know what all the engineers are saying. How will anyone reading the plan know what we are saying about our product is true? The answer is that they won't. But if they are really concerned about that, and they intend to lend you the money or invest in your company, they will go through a process called "due diligence" in which they will check out the claims you have made about your product (and about your market, your customers, your finances, your employees and many other things). Again, the information in your business plan should include a brief (very brief) description of your technology only to the degree that your technology provides an advantage vis-à-vis the competition.

What you do need to spend a whole lot of time on, in your business plan, is how you get your product to market. Lenders and investors will generally take your word that your products do what you say they do. If they are really interested in funding your company, they may ask for specific proof on product claims; however, often, the work of verifying product claims is left to due diligence staff, and in some cases, third-party consultants. I worked with one lender that basically outsourced their entire due diligence process to a third-party due diligence company (of course, we had to pay upfront for those guys to do their work). But long before you get to that stage, you need to convince the decision-makers that you know what you're doing, and that means demonstrating you understand your markets, you understand the distribution systems in those markets, and you have a plan for getting your product into those distribution streams, or in the case of companies that are simply expanding, have an understanding of how the market works and how most effectively to increase sales.

The facts are that having a better mousetrap does not necessarily create sales. Most of us remember some product we bought in the past years, which we thought highly of, but which seemed to disappear from the market later. And further, if we look at successful companies, most will agree that those companies are not necessarily the best in their industries. But there is one thing those companies do understand—how to market their services and, as important, what drives the buying decisions of their target customers. You need to be able to demonstrate in your plan that you understand how to market to your target customers, and how your target customers make purchasing decisions. I see this area so poorly covered in business plans; it is incredible. Yet this is far more important than thirty pages describing your great products. Closely related to this issue is the CEO who thinks he knows how the market works, but in fact, his viewpoints are all biased by his own personal opinions and value systems. Some graduate-degreed executive, living in the better part of town, driving a BMW, who eats at Morton's, better have some pretty good independent research before making the claim that he understands what drives the buying decisions of nineteen-year-old single mothers.

When preparing your business plan, take some time to make sure your business plan answers these key questions:

[handwritten margin note: How many decisions does a grower do in a season?]

- Who are your customers now, and who will they be in the future?
- How do your customers make decisions to buy your products or similar products?
- How long does it take target customers to make decisions to buy your product and/or to switch

[handwritten note: In Ag it can be +1 year!]

from those products they are currently using?
- How do competitors of your business market their products?
- How do you plan to market your products?
- What is/are the motivating factor(s) that would make a customer change from the product he is currently using, to your product?
- Why is there a need for your product?
- How is your product delivered to the customer?

There are many more questions that you could ask, but hopefully, you get the idea. Your plan needs to cover your customers, your market, the distribution system for your products, what motivates and drives customers, and why the market needs your product. If you can communicate that message effectively, you have a much greater chance of getting a funding source to take a second look at your business.

The right length. This is a simple point, but your business plan needs to be the right length. Clearly, some businesses are more complex than others. Therefore, some business plans need to be more complex and more thorough than others. Don't fill your business plan with filler and irrelevant information if the sole purpose of the additional information is just to add pages. How do you know what is relevant and irrelevant? A lot of this is just common sense. If you have five hundred customers, listing sales by customer is something that should not be in your business plan. However, if you have five hundred customers and Walmart accounts for 50 percent of your sales, that's a fact you should mention. While there are no strict rules, a business plan of five pages is probably too short. There is probably too much information missing.

On the other hand, a business plan of 150 pages is probably too long. It probably contains too much information that is not relevant to the business plan itself—information that is more tactical than strategic. Your best way to handle length is to have the plan reviewed by someone who is independent and who will be honest with you and tell you if it does a good job of telling your story and if it has holes in it. I have seen excellent business plans of eight to ten pages that did a great job of explaining the company's business, its competitive advantages, and why the company will be successful.

Financial projections. When we talk about business plans, there is some confusion between the written part of the business plan and the financial projections. I have asked people to send me their business plans in the past, and, on enough occasions to notice, I have gotten a written plan without financial projections, and in some cases, have gotten nothing but financial projections. So, what, if any, financial information should be included in your business plan? And, what is the relationship between the projections and the plan itself? The financial projections are a result of the business plan. By financial projections, I am talking about a financial model, usually prepared using some sort of spreadsheet program like Excel. The written plan comes first, so projections without a written plan are not appropriate. You could send someone your business plan without your financial projections (and in most cases, that is what I would recommend). Still, you should never send anyone your financial projections without your business plan.

The business plan is where you develop the assumptions upon which your financial projections are based. Then you put together the projections using those assumptions. Depending upon the complexity of your financial model, you may include all of your financial projections in the business plan document, but typically the business plan only includes a summary of the financial projections, having your complete financial projections as a separate document that you probably would provide subsequent to providing the business plan and perhaps even after your first meeting (see Chapter "Assumption Driven Financial Models" for more information on financial projections). To clarify what I am talking about, your business plan might include summary income statements going out three to five years. Your financial model that developed those income statements might include fifteen different spreadsheets where you developed customer-based sales projections, expense models, employee lists, and other detailed information. You would not normally include that level of detailed financial information in your business plan.

However, you do need to have detailed financial projections, and you need to understand the model, so if you aren't a financial guy, or if you hired some spreadsheet wiz to prepare your financial model, make sure you understand it well enough to be able to explain it to a money guy or his analyst when the need arises. That may seem obvious, but I have met many CEOs who left the financial modeling to their CFO and could not answer basic questions about assumptions used in developing those projections. Regardless of who prepares the financial projections, money guys expect the CEO to be knowledgeable enough to explain the projections and answer questions related to the assumptions therein.

Your business plan is a living document. That means that as your business develops, your business plan will constantly be changing. The best business plans are those that change as the authors of the business plan—the leaders of the company—learn more information about their business, their market, their competitors, and the economy. Some of the best ideas for business plans come from people who may be reviewing your business plan when looking to lend you money or invest in your business. Listen to what they say. Don't argue with them or try to defend your position (this is something we will talk more about later on and is extremely important)! Take every question you get about your business as an opportunity to rethink the way you are approaching the business, and every suggestion as an opportunity to improve your plan, and the way you plan to do business.

I have worked with CEOs of fledgling enterprises and CEOs of mature companies that have been around for many years—profitable companies, unprofitable companies, fast-growth companies, stagnant companies, and floundering companies—and my one universal observation is that most CEOs and other senior executives are so entrenched in their industry perspective, their personal experience, and their personal (emotional) investment in their world view, that they have ceased to benefit from all of the great learning experiences we find in every conversation. I think this is one of the reasons why so much innovation comes from outsiders, not from industry leaders, because it's just too tough to challenge one's own thoughts, ideas, and beliefs. There are a million great ideas to help you with your business, available for free, just by listening intently to the thoughts and ideas of others. Take advantage of all those free ideas by listening and by being open-minded.

I recommend you write your business in a Word document. However, today many businesses put together a business plan "deck." The deck is a PowerPoint presentation that replaces a written word document. Note: there is a difference between this deck and the pitch deck we will discuss later. The business plan deck includes the well-crafted business plan reduced to bullet points and short paragraphs, with plenty of pictures and graphics. This type of business plan is increasingly being used because people simply do not read as much as they used to. In fact, many younger people have difficulty reading something that is mostly text. Ever have a look at today's university textbooks? They are filled with pictures, sidebars, comment boxes, and other graphic tools to make reading easier. The PowerPoint business plan is designed to be read (as opposed to supporting an oral presentation), but it includes enough pictures and graphics that it is visually appealing to the reader. I know it is extra work, but I recommend that you have both available. Also, once you have completed your written plan, go through it and add pictures, graphics, borders, and other document enhancements that make it more readable. This way, you will have two versions of your plan to share – a more traditional written plan in a Word document and a summary of that plan with pictures and graphics in a PowerPoint (or PDF) document.

My final point on business plans is that creating a business plan is also a process of creating a viable business. In the process of developing a business plan, you will have to perform research, consider alternatives, and choose between options. Even if you have the entire plan and strategy mapped out in your head (which many business leaders do), putting it down on paper (or should I say putting it into an electronic document) is a good method of improving and refining the plan and making sure you haven't overlooked obvious weaknesses that might be easily spotted by investors.

Summary of Business Plans Dos and Don'ts

- Make sure you use correct spelling and grammar.
- Make sure your plan is consistent from one section to the next.
- Tie in all the numbers, particularly between the written text and the financial projections.
- Clearly articulate your company's distribution system.
- Explain clearly how you get your product to market, or how you plan to get your product to market.
- Don't get too technical or spend too much time on the technical side of your products.
- Talk a lot about your customers and what will drive them to buy your product over the competition.
- Talk a lot about the markets and your competition.
- Hire a professional to write your plan if you are not willing to invest the time and effort to do it yourself.
- If you do it yourself, look at other plans or books on how to write business plans for ideas and examples.
- Make it the right length—not too short and not too long.
- Include summary projections, but not your entire financial model.
- Don't miss the opportunity to change and modify your plan based on the feedback you get from anyone who reads it.
- Prepare both a Word and PowerPoint version.

ASSUMPTIONS ARE EVERYTHING

This chapter is about financial projections, but I named it *Assumptions Are Everything* because financial projections are only as good as the assumptions you make when you build those projections. First, let's get one thing clear – you need to have a set of financial projections. My recommendation is that those projections should go out five years on a month-by-month basis, and need to include income statements, balance sheets, and statements of cash flow.

My experience is that while many management teams can put together a pretty good business plan and investor deck, most management teams do a very poor job on financial projections. It may be that I am overly critical because I am a finance guy and a CFO, but to me, the financial projections tell a story – and poor projections tell a poor story.

So how do you create great financial projections? Much of your financial projections should be based on information included in your business plan about products, customers, and markets. The first thing you forecast is sales revenue. Everything else in your projections is driven off sales revenue. But sales revenue must be based on logical "revenue drivers." Many times I will open a set of financial projections, look at the sales forecast, then move my cursor over the cell for sales in month one, and see that whoever prepared the forecast simply typed in a number "10,000." Projections prepared in this fashion are considered amateurish, and many money guys will lose interest the minute they see such poorly prepared projections.

So how do you prepare projections? Go back to your business plan to look at the research you did on the size of the market, market growth, what you are selling, and how you will market what you are selling. With that information in hand, you should be able to build a revenue assumption table.

Let me give you an example. Let's say you've developed a new type of coffee maker that you think will be perfect for hotel rooms. You think it will sell into other markets too, but your main focus will be on hotel rooms because you can't tackle every market at once. In preparing your business plan, you did some research and found out the following information:

- There are 5 million hotel rooms in the United States

- Approximately 80% of hotel rooms provide an in-room coffee maker
- The average hotel room gets renovated every seven years.
- The annual growth rate in new hotel rooms is 4%.
- Approximately 5% of coffee makers need to be replaced each year.
- There are two main competitors. Each competitor holds about 45% of the market, with the other 10% being held by several different suppliers.

Okay, you now have the information off which you can begin to build your model. You still need to figure out two additional pieces of information: How much of the market you can capture and what kind of revenue growth rates you can achieve. In this case, let's assume you can achieve about 3% market penetration in year one, and sales should grow by 12% per month for at least the first two years. You also have determined that the selling price will be \$22 per unit and that your cost of goods will be \$8 per unit. With this information, you can build an "assumption-based model." The first thing you do is lay out your assumptions in a table on Excel. See the example below.

Assumptions			
# Hotel rooms in the US			5,000,000
% with coffee makers			80%
Years between renovations			7
Replacement coffee makers			5%
Growth in Hotel Rooms annually			4%
Selling Price			22
COGS			8
Market Share month one			0.87%
Revenue growth per month			12%

From this table, you can build a month-to-month projection.

	Mo 1	Mo 2	Mo 3	Mo 4	Mo 5	Mo 6
Market Size of Hotel Rooms	5,000,000	5,016,667	5,033,389	5,050,167	5,067,001	5,083,891
Renovations Each Month	47,619	47,778	47,937	48,097	48,257	48,418
Replacement Coffee Maker	16,667	16,722	16,778	16,834	16,890	16,946
Market Size for Coffee Makers	64,286	64,500	64,715	64,931	65,147	65,364
Market Share	0.87%	0.97%	1.09%	1.22%	1.37%	1.53%
Sales in Units	559	628	706	794	892	1,002
Sales in Dollars	12,304	13,827	15,538	17,460	19,620	22,048
COGS	4,474	5,028	5,650	6,349	7,135	8,018
Gross Profit	7,830	8,799	9,888	11,111	12,486	14,031

If you had access to the actual Excel file, you would see that all the numbers in the month-to-month projections are formula-driven using the information from the assumptions table. I only included the first six months, but in the model I built for this example, I take the numbers out for five years on a month-to-month basis. You need to build your model based on the revenue drivers for your business, which could be subscriptions, sales per click, sales per dollar of advertising spent, sales per square feet, and so on.

Once you have built your revenue assumptions, you need to build your expense assumptions. Most expenses have expense drivers. You figure out what those expense drivers are and build them into your assumptions page. Warehouse space might be driven by the size of your inventory, and marketing could be a percentage of sales, insurance could be a percentage of sales, fulfillment could be based on units shipped, and so on. Some expenses may stay constant regardless of revenue, so you build that into your model as well. But every possible expense, including payroll, marketing, and operations, should be driven off your assumptions table.

When you build your model, I recommend you have the following schedules in your Excel workbook (obviously, certain business types will not need all of these schedules so you must tailor your schedules to your business):

Summary income statements, balance sheets and statement of cash flows
Detailed income statements, balance sheets and statement of cash flows
Sales revenue by product and unit schedule
Inventory schedule
Human capital schedule
Operating expense schedule
Fixed asset and depreciation schedule
Debt schedule.

When the projections are built off of assumptions, we say the model is assumption drive, whereas if the numbers are typed into each cell, we refer to the numbers as being "hardwired." Why do we want the numbers assumption-driven? It is simple. Because an assumption-driven model allows us to change one number and see the impact that change has on the entire projections, so as an example, after preparing my model, I look to see how my revenue will track based on a month-to-month growth rate of 12%. In month six, I am only selling 1,002 units. I think I can do better than that based on some preliminary discussions with a couple of hotel supply companies. If I go change my growth rate to 20%, then my entire model changes accordingly. I have built models that contain as many as 60 or 70 assumptions. It seems like a lot of work, but when some money guy says, "Well, what if your customer acquisition cost is $40, not $30? How will that affect working capital?" you will be able to answer the question in a couple of seconds.

The other benefit of assumption driven models is it really gets you thinking about how you need to build out your business to support your revenue objectives. How many employees will you need? What positions will they fill? How much inventory must you carry? How much office and warehouse space will you need? The answers to so many of these questions come from your financial projections. They become a great business-planning tool.

A few more points on projections. As you are building them, continually review them for what I call the "reasonableness test." Do the numbers really make sense? As an example, I saw the projection for a business that planned to sell a product into the educational market. The owner predicted that each salesperson would achieve a specified dollar amount of sales. However, to achieve his sales projections, he would have to hire over 100 salespeople in the first year of operations. That would be a real challenge for most companies, to hire and train over 100 salespeople in year one. Another mistake people make in preparing projections is an ever-increasing revenue line, with a much smaller increasing cost line. Yes, you will get certain economies of scale as time goes by, but as your organization grows, so do your expenses. Projecting huge profit margins in years three, four, and five are typically met with a lot of skepticism.

People often ask me if they can use one of those "template" financial models that you can purchase off the Internet. My experience with those models is that many of them don't have the flexibility to adapt to many different types of business models, and varying business circumstances. Further, many of them do not allow for the detail I believe is needed in good models. You will do much better to build the model yourself, although if you are pressed for time and looking at it as a starting point, using a template can at least get you something, if you currently have nothing.

My final point on models is that if you don't have the Excel and accounting skills to build the model yourself, hire someone who does. It will be money well spent. But don't think if you are the CEO that you can leave the model-building to your CFO, accountant, or some contract worker. That person is going to provide the model architecture – it is your job to understand how the model works and to be able to support in a reasonable manner every assumption you have used in the model.

SNAPSHOT

As you are developing your business plan, or if you already have a business plan, you need to develop two additional valuable items in your arsenal of fund-raising tools. Those items are what I call the "two-pager" and the "pitch." The two-pager is a two-page summary of your business plan and is a very useful tool to get money sources interested in your business. The pitch is your oral version of the two-pager, designed to give the person you are pitching a quick idea of what your deal is all about, and entice them to go the next step—either have a meeting or allow you to send them more complete information.

I have had many hundreds of people ask me to help them raise capital over the years, and most fund managers, lenders, investment bankers, and other capital sources have shared this same experience. This is a typical scenario. My phone rings...

"Hello."

"Hi. My name's Jack Burns. Grant over at ABC Capital told me to give you a call... Said you might be able to help me. I'm looking for some money for my business."

Now, I love talking to people about their business. New business or a mature business, profitable or in trouble, it doesn't matter. I always see possibilities in a business, and I get excited in thinking about how I can help a business get to the next stage. So, my next comment would be.

"Okay, Jack, tell me a little bit about your business and how I can help you."

"Sure. Well, my dad came back from the war in '45. He went in with the first wave on Iwo Jima and spent three months on that bloody island. Unfortunately, he got his left foot blown off, so that was it for him. But he did get a Bronze Star, and I have that Bronze Star hanging on my office wall, and I think about my dad every day."

I interrupt, trying to get to the point. "So, Jack, your dad started a business framing memorabilia for returning veterans. Sounds like a great idea."

"No…ha-ha…nothing like that. In fact, without that foot, my dad couldn't go into anything that required him to walk too much, so he went back to college under the G.I. bill and became an accountant. A lot of his customers were fellow G.I.s."

"Great," I said, "you have a business that specializes in providing financial services to veterans. Sounds like a good market niche."

"No, no…nothing like that. But let me finish."

By now, I'm ready to pull out my hair. I don't have all day to listen to Jack's stories. I have a million calls to make, and I'm late for a meeting.

"Tell you what, Jack. Here's my email address. Send me an email with a summary of your business, and we'll talk a little later. Sorry to cut it short, but I've got a meeting just about to start."

Three hours later, I check my email. There is an email from Jack, and it includes an eighty-page business plan, a fifty-page PowerPoint presentation, PDF files of the company's financial statements, and a PDF file of a U.S. patent. Jack's message says, "Review this information and check out my Website at www.wasteoftime.com, and then let's talk."

I file the email under "Prospects," thinking that when I have some time I'll look at it, but then I get busy and never do. Two weeks later, Jack calls me back, and the conversation goes like this.

"Hello."

"Hey, it's Jack. What do you think about my business?"

"Well, Jack. I don't think I can do anything with this one. But thanks for thinking of me and let me know how you make out."

What happened here? It's simple. No funding source has the time or interest in reviewing pages and pages of material on your business. Investment bankers and business bank lenders get hundreds of packages of information a week. Most of it never even gets a cursory glance unless it relates to a deal for which they have specifically requested additional information.

To make it interesting, you need to be able to present your business in a snapshot. Ideally, you should be able to do that both orally and in written form. The best way to develop your oral "pitch" is to prepare a written two-page summary from your business plan. Then, from your two-page summary, you can boil the summary down into a three or four minute pitch.

To be able to deliver what your company is all about in less than five minutes is essential. From my experience, if you are pitching your deal orally, the decision to move to the next step (a meeting, looking at your business plan, etc.) happens in the first five minutes. Someone may listen to you for fifteen minutes to be polite, but if you haven't piqued their interest in the first five, you've probably lost them.

A few years back, I was in one those overly priced cocktail lounges in Newport Beach, sipping on my $15 martini and watching the cosmetic surgery patients trying to pick up millionaires in the bar, when a friend of mine pulled over a gentleman in his late fifties and introduced him to me. Apparently, the individual was a retired airline pilot of some notoriety, and now that he was retired, he had developed a business concept relating to aviation. I was all ears.

"So, tell me about your business," I said.

He stared me in the eye, a very serious look on his face. "I would love to. But first, I need you to sign a non-disclosure agreement" (we'll talk more about these later).

"Well, that's kind of hard to do in the bar. Just give me the high-level version, and don't tell me anything that's really proprietary or confidential."

He said, "I guess I could do it that way. Do you have about an hour?"

I look at him in amazement. "No, just give me an overview. You know...the five-minute version."

He frowned and shook his head. "There's no way to explain my business in five minutes. We'll do it another time when you can give me forty-five minutes to an hour. Otherwise, you'll never understand what my business is all about."

Now, I'm telling you, any business on the planet can be described in five minutes, and any business owner who needs an hour to describe his business is never going to get funding!! So, use my concept of developing a two-page summary and then turning that into an oral pitch, and you'll have an easy way to describe your business in five minutes.

Whether you get a capital source's interest from your oral pitch, or from your two-pager, understand the two work hand in hand. If you get the opportunity to give your oral pitch, you back it up with your two-pager. If you don't get the opportunity to give your oral pitch, the two-pager provides a document that can be scanned in five minutes. If I get something in my email that is going to take five minutes to read, I probably will read it. If I get an eighty-page business plan, I probably will not.

So, what does your pitch and your two-pager look like? I've included a couple of examples below. The two-pager begins with the *investment highlights* (in the following two examples, these companies were looking for equity investments, but this same format can easily be adapted for a company looking for debt). The *investment highlights* or more simply, the *highlights*, are those key phrases that are designed to perk up the ears of the person reading the two-pager, or listening to your pitch, and make them think this is a company worth taking a second look at, enticing them to read the rest of the two-pager to get the full story.

The next section is the *business overview*—a one-paragraph summary of your business that focuses on your core strategy and competitive advantages. The two-pager also should include the *opportunity*, which includes information on the product, the market, and the competition. The information you include in your two-pager will vary depending upon your business, but the idea is to boil down your business plan into two pages of the most relevant and meaningful information on your company so that a reader, by reading your two-pager, could have a pretty clear understanding of your business and what your business does. Whenever you give your pitch, always follow it up with a printed or emailed copy of your two-pager. Print up a few copies of the two-pager on 8.5" x 11" paper, fold them in a trifold, and keep a few in your jacket pocket to hand to people. When looking at my samples, you may think they are more than two pages, but in fact, by putting in very small margins and using smaller font sizes, both these examples fit perfectly on two pages. My examples do not include pictures. If you can add pictures and nice graphics to your two-pager, all the better. Perhaps change some of the paragraphs to bullet points to reduce the text and allow you to add more pictures. Of course, make sure any pictures or graphs you add are related to your business. Adding pictures just to have pictures does not help, but relevant pictures can really make your two-pager look impressive. Years ago, I would not have been concerned about pictures, but today they will help with your presentation.

Your oral pitch comes right off the information on your two-pager. When you pitch the deal orally, you give the *business overview* first, the *opportunity* second, and the *investment highlights* last. When giving your pitch, remember that you cannot read it. When you read something, it is obvious to the listener. So, after you have prepared your two-pager, take the highlights, the overview, and the opportunity and put them into a separate document in bullet format. Then practice giving the pitch using the bullet points as guidelines. After a few tries, the flow of the pitch will become natural, and you will be able to give your five-minute pitch, including an overview of the business, review of the opportunity, and a summary of the highlights in an effective and convincing manner.

If you are not a good speaker, practice your pitch in front of the mirror or in front of friends, or even videotape your pitch and play it back. The more easily and smoothly you can give this five-minute pitch, the more effective you will become at getting the interest of the money guys.

Remember, the pitch is not to be used when you give a formal presentation or when a previous meeting has been arranged. The pitch is what you use when you are making cold calls to funding sources, when you meet someone at a cocktail party or event, or when you are introduced to someone, and your first contact is expected to be brief.

The two-pager is something that you keep in your briefcase and in a computer file, and you hand it out to people you meet casually (such as at an event) or email it to people you talk with on the phone as a follow up to your conversation (a conversation in which we are assuming you gave your well-honed pitch).

In reviewing the two examples, note one thing further. These two examples do not include a company name. I always recommend you prepare two versions of your two-pager. One is a "blind" copy that does not include the company names or other information that would allow the reader to identify the company. The other is a copy that does include the company name and perhaps other information that would allow the reader to identify the company. The blind version allows you to gain more exposure for your deal without the worry about getting non-disclosure agreements signed (again, we'll talk more about these later) or having too many people know who it is that is actually looking for the money.

Also, note that the two-pager does not have to be exactly two pages. It can be a little longer, or a little shorter. But it should be approximately two pages, because in two pages you can give enough information for someone to really understand the gist of your business, and it is short enough to be read very quickly, which respects people's time and also increases the likelihood it will be read.

<u>Two-pager Example 1</u>

Aircraft Leasing Company

Confidential Executive Summary

Investment Highlights:

➢ Increasing demand for aircraft as air transportation fleets expected to double in 20 years

➢ Increasing demand for aircraft leases pushed by low-cost carriers
➢ Uniquely positioned to lever key industry relationships - UTX and Pratt & Whitney
➢ "Ahead of market" opportunities created by sister companies
➢ Limited competition due to substantial barriers to entry
➢ Seasoned management with significant industry experience
➢ Above-average returns fueled by the low cost of operations compared to competitors

Business Overview

Aircraft Leasing Company ("ALC") is in the business of purchasing, leasing, and trading commercial aircraft, spare engines, and spare part pools. Its strategy is to build a portfolio of aircraft and engine leases with an emphasis on 15- to 25-year-old, single-aisle industry workhorses, such as 737s and A320s. ALC is uniquely positioned as a new entrant into this industry due to its common ownership with two aviation services companies ("ASCs"). ASCs, co-located in common facilities at a major airport, provide a range of services to commercial air carriers, including recovery, evaluation, maintenance, storage, reconfiguration, reactivation, marketing, lease placement, and lease management services. ASCs, formed in 1999 and approximately 50% owned by a major publicly-traded company since 2002, have provided services to a stellar list of airline industry titans (Boeing, GE, United, Delta, CIT, and Federal Express) and have been engaged in aircraft transactions with assets valued in the billions of dollars. ALC intends to produce annual sales of $115 million by the year 2011, and to generate EBIT of $72 million.

The Industry

Two significant trends are creating an increased demand for commercial aircraft and commercial aircraft leasing opportunities. World air travel continues to grow—having grown in 32 of the last 35 years, and with Boeing predicting annual worldwide passenger growth of 4.9% and worldwide cargo traffic growth of 6.1%, through 2025. The growing demand for air travel will result in a worldwide fleet of approximately 36,000 airplanes in 2025, double the current number of commercial airplanes.

Low-cost carriers are driving industry expansion. Accounting for 12% U.S. market share in 1995, low-cost carriers had captured 27% by 2004. In Europe, low-cost carriers jumped from less than 1% in 1995 to 17% in 2004. These low-cost carriers are driving the market for single-aisle aircraft (737 and A320 types), which are expected to comprise 61% of the global aircraft fleet by 2024, and account for 92% of the total world departures.

At the same time, as demand is increasing for single-aisle aircraft (ALC's target market), the demand for leased aircraft is also on the rise. In 1996, leases accounted for 19% of total aircraft, with 42% of airlines operating entirely on leased aircraft. In 2005, approximately one-third of all commercial aircraft were leased, with 75% of the 600 worldwide airlines using operating leases for some or all their fleet.

Leasing mirrors today's business trend of outsourcing. Airlines are looking to do what has the most effect on the bottom line—filling seats with paying customers or cargo holds with freight. Through leasing, airlines can better leverage their financial resources, expand fleet size more readily, potentially obtain certain tax advantages, and adapt more quickly to changing market opportunities.

Product

ALC provides its services primarily in the form of operating leases. An operating lease means that the lessor (that would be ALC) retains ownership of the asset and rents it to the airline for an agreed period of time, typically 3 to 5 years. These agreements are generally net leases, whereby the lessee is responsible for all operating expenses, including maintenance, taxes, and insurance. Rental payments are structured into two parts—the base rent, with a fixed monthly fee, and a variable fee contingent upon the lessees' flying hours, which are commonly referred to as a maintenance reserve. ALC intends to operate leases primarily on 737 and A320 class aircraft, of between 15 and 25 years old, and engines for such aircraft. The Company may write leases on other models of aircraft depending upon market opportunity and circumstance. The Company's leasing products are like those of other aircraft leasing companies due to the nature and size of the industry.

Markets and Competition

ALC's target market is easily stated—commercial air carriers that operate leased aircraft. This represents approximately 400 air carriers worldwide. Within that market segment, ALC intends to focus on second and third-tier carriers, which would include newer carriers, small carriers, and foreign carriers.

Competition for air carriers worldwide comes primarily from two sources—financial institutions and intermediaries. Financial institutions include such groups as GECAS and ILFC that engage in aircraft leasing. These companies are characterized by the availability of extremely large pools of capital and focus on new aircraft leases to major carriers. Intermediaries are typically middlemen, who act as go-betweens between available aircraft and potential customers. The key to success for intermediaries is access to the product (aircraft being sold, put into storage, and coming off lease) and access to customers (air carriers interested in expanding their fleets). Due to the nature of the industry, getting into the supply and demand pipeline is extremely difficult, and poses a substantial barrier to entry for new market participants.

ALC ranks as an intermediary. However, ALC has a significant competitive advantage over most intermediaries. Through its relationship with the ASCs, ALC is made aware of product opportunities before other intermediaries, as the ASCs are in constant contact with air carrier fleet managers, and in many cases, processing aircraft for these fleet managers that are being transitioned. At the same time, through its affiliation with a major publicly traded company, and the worldwide network of that company's subsidiaries is in contact with fleet managers across the globe in search of the product. Through the incoming business and the outbound connections of the ASCs, and the major public company, ALC is uniquely positioned to pair the available product with customer demand, and at a significantly lower marketing and administrative cost than its competition through the shared resources of these related and synergistic entities.

Financial Projections (in millions)

YEAR	2007	2008	2009	2010	2011
REVENUE	19.2	31.7	50	75.4	114.8
EBIT	9.3	17.6	28.7	44	71.7

Investment Opportunity:

ALC is offering a 35% interest in the company for $25 million. The offering is for 250,000 units at $100 per unit, with a minimum investment of $25,000. Purchasers will receive an annual distribution of 25% of profit before tax, with a projected 50% of profit before tax paid to investors by the year 2011. The Company anticipates that a liquidity event will be precipitated by the ALC going public or being acquired by a large player in the aviation industry. The Company also provides put rights, exercisable in 2011, 2012, and 2013, in which ALC would repurchase, at appraised value, an electing investor's units over a fixed time period. Based on management's estimates, investors will achieve an approximately 39% average annual return on investment.

* * *

Two-pager Example 2

Specialty Lubricant Company

Confidential Executive Summary

Investment Highlights

➤ Increasing demand for environmentally friendly products that reduce energy consumption
➤ Money-saving products that significantly extend the life of machinery and equipment
➤ "Next-generation" products that outperform the competition by a substantial margin
➤ Proprietary formulations with high margins in a $10 billion market
➤ Huge international opportunity (recently signed $75 million distribution agreement in China)
➤ Stability of commercial/industrial market *plus* huge upside in direct response and retail markets
➤ Products shipping today as Company is poised for explosive growth

Business Overview

The Company is in the business of developing and marketing high-performance, cost-effective, "friction reduction" products for commercial, industrial, and retail customers. The product family includes a new generation of advanced lubricants, greases, fuel additives, cutting oils, spray lubricants, hydraulic fluids, and automotive cleaners. The products are proprietary formulations based upon metallurgical and molecular science that reduce friction substantially better than other products on the market, with over 50 times the film strength of conventional lubricants. In addition to the economic benefits of longer equipment life, lower maintenance costs, and less lubricant consumption, the Company's products are great for the environment as they reduce the consumption of natural resources, such as electricity, fossil fuels, and water. With the growing demand in a $10 billion market for environmentally friendly, high-performance lubricant products, the Company is well-positioned for exponential growth and profitability.

The Industry

The Company's products fall primarily into the lubricants, fuel additives, and automotive maintenance industry classification, a $10 billion per year market. This segment includes a wide variety of lubricant product types, including engine oils, transmission oils, hydraulic fluids, gear oils, industrial lubricants, cutting oils, metalworking lubricants, greases, fuel treatments, and automotive cleaners. The market is both stable and trending upward at a steady and predictable pace.

Three significant trends drive demand for the Company's advanced friction reduction products. First, the cost of machinery and equipment has skyrocketed. Computer controls, improved functionality, increased government regulation, and new metal compounds have increased the cost of everything from industrial diesel engines to CNC production-line equipment. Today's factories, airports, transportation systems, and office buildings run on expensive, sophisticated machines. Owners and operators focus on maintenance strategies that reduce downtime and increase equipment life. Advanced friction reduction products fill this need. Second, operators of machinery are increasingly under scrutiny from environmental watchdogs and subject to a host of federal, state, and local government regulations designed to reduce toxic waste and energy consumption. Earth-friendly advanced friction reduction products play a vital role in accomplishing such environmental objectives. Third, rising oil prices and a worldwide energy shortage have put tremendous pressure on the commercial fleet, manufacturing, and mining sectors to reduce energy consumption. The reduction in friction by using the Company's lubricants makes automobile and truck engines run more efficiently, optimizing fuel economy, while the Company's industrial lubricants increase machinery efficiency, resulting in the equipment drawing less power.

Products

The Company has a broad line of products designed to reduce friction between moving parts and create cost and environmental benefits. Since man first rubbed two objects together, he has been searching for ways to reduce friction. Friction is the surface resistance that occurs when two objects rub together. Friction creates heat and wear. Whether pistons in a car engine, cutting tools on a CNC machine, or ball bearings on a bicycle, friction will eventually break down every moving part of every gadget and machine that man has ever made.

The Company's proprietary formulas reduce friction better than anything else on the market. Traditional lubrication products break down as heat and pressure rise and migrate away from the source of friction (causing excessive wear at the point of contact). The Company's advanced friction reduction formulas migrate toward heat and pressure, and literally bond with metal and other materials at the point of contact. The effect of this bonding is a microscopic layer of molecules rubbing against another microscopic layer of molecules, protecting the component parts from grinding against each other. The result: friction is reduced, the energy required to move those parts is reduced, and the parts (and the lubricant) last longer. The benefits: lower operating costs, reduced fuel and lubricant consumption, and extended machine life. **On a value analysis basis, the cost savings benefit of the Company's products significantly outweighs the premium price they command in the marketplace.**

Markets and Competition

The market for the Company's products is worldwide and extends to virtually every operator of equipment and machinery. The Company is distributing domestically through industrial and commercial distributors and reps (for example, Fastenal with 2,200 industrial supply outlets and 3,000 direct sales reps). Internationally, the Company is establishing master distributors, and has just signed an agreement for distribution in China with a minimum commitment of $75 million in sales over the life of the agreement. The Company will also distribute some of its products through direct response marketing, and ultimately through major retail chains, such as Pep Boys, AutoZone, Home Depot, etc. The consumer products alone could generate as much as $100 million in sales in the next 24 to 36 months.

Competition for the Company's products comes primarily from two sources—major fossil-fuel-based oil companies like Pennzoil and Chevron, and niche product manufacturers like WD-40 and Master Chemical. There is no competitor; however, that commands a dominant market share in any of the lubricant product classifications (grease, spray lube, cutting oil, hydraulic oil, fuel additives, etc.). **More importantly, in head-to-head testing in both the lab and in real-life applications, the Company's products outperform the competition in every category by a wide margin.**

Financial Projections (in millions)

YEAR	2008	2009	2010
Revenue	13.2	32.4	46.4
Gross Profit	5.6	14.9	21.7
EBIT	0.7	3.9	6.9

Investment Opportunity

The Company is seeking expansion capital of approximately $3 million. The proceeds will be used primarily for working capital (investment in inventory and accounts receivable) and for product marketing, including launching the company's major consumer product through a direct response marketing campaign. The company recently merged into a non-reporting public company, but intends to begin reporting as quickly as possible, and move from the "pink sheets" to the OTCBB.

* * *

`A VISUAL STORY LINE

At some point in time, if you get someone interested in possibly funding your deal, the funding source is going to want to meet management and hear a presentation to learn more about the business. Presentations typically involve a meeting with a member, or members, of the company's management team, and a member, or members, of the funding source's decision-makers. Such meetings can take place at the company's offices, at the funding source's offices, or even at a neutral location such as a conference facility, restaurant, or the airport. I have some very specific and valuable information on how to conduct such meetings, but this chapter focuses specifically on one part of these introductory meetings—the PowerPoint presentation.

Remember I mentioned previously that I recommend you prepare a PowerPoint formatted business plan (see "Business Plans"). The PowerPoint I am describing here is not the same. What you ask? Do I need two PowerPoints? Well, that is up to you. You may decide you will not have a business plan Power-Point, but only a Word document business plan. I recommend both. But you absolutely need a PowerPoint presentation, and the PowerPoint presentation differs from the business plan PowerPoint as described below.

Typically, when looking for funds, a company prepares a PowerPoint presentation. These presentations serve two useful purposes. They keep the discussion focused on the business, its plans, opportunities, and strengths. And it also provides the presenter with a roadmap or guidebook when telling the company's story, so that all the key highlights and elements are covered. Unfortunately, a poorly crafted and presented Power-Point presentation can scuttle an otherwise great deal. There are two sets of rules relating to PowerPoint presentations. The first set of rules relates to how you prepare the PowerPoint presentation and its contents. The second set of rules relates to how you present the PowerPoint presentation. Let's talk about preparing the PowerPoint presentation. This chapter covers the first set of rules. The next chapter will cover the second set of rules.

Keep it short. I attended an investment conference, and one of the presenters was the CEO of a biotech company that had raised over $100 million for research into some new drugs. At this conference, each speaker had twenty minutes to speak, then five minutes for Q & A, and then there was a five-minute break while the next presentation was loaded, and the next group of speakers got up on stage. When this CEO got up and turned on his PowerPoint presentation, before he started the slide show, I noticed that his presentation had sixty-three slides. Do the math. That means he had approximately nineteen seconds to present each slide. And of course, he was a rambling windbag, and by the time he got to two minutes left, (they ring a little warning bell); he still had thirty slides to go. You should have seen him try to cram those last thirty slides, many of which were very technical and full of formulas and equations, into those two minutes. He came across as disorganized and disjointed, and I thought to myself, "How did this buffoon ever manage to raise $100 million?" Worse, at the end of his presentation, I still didn't have a clue as to what his business was really trying to do.

I used to recommend that your PowerPoint presentation

should have no more than twenty to twenty-five slides, and that includes the title page, and maybe a summary slide. That meant about eighteen to twenty-three slides that contain content about which you can talk. My thinking was that if you spend one minute on each slide, you'll have an eighteen to twenty-three-minute presentation, which is just about perfect. If your presentation goes any longer than twenty-five minutes, you'll begin to lose your audience. We'll talk about timing more when we discuss the rules for giving your presentation.

However, times have changed. A presentation that is eighteen to twenty-three slides long, I now consider too long. Attention spans continue to shorten, and even professional investors will quickly get bored with a presentation of that length. Today I am recommending a presentation of no more than ten to twelve slides, including a cover slide and a summary slide. If you can do it in eight slides, even better. It may mean you talk a little more when each slide is on the screen, or you allow more time for questions, but keeping it short and delivering a sharp, concise presentation will be much better at keeping the attention of the audience. Remember, for many of them, even fifteen minutes without checking their cell phones for text messages is a long time, and when they are looking at the screen on their cell phones, they are not listening to you.

Keep slide content to a minimum. The purpose of the PowerPoint slide is to give the presenter a reference point and highlight the most important or critical messages you want to convey relating to that segment of the presentation. Many preparers of PowerPoint presentations make the mistake of writing their speech—everything they intend to say—on the slide so that the PowerPoint presentation looks more like a book. Here is an example of a poorly crafted slide.

Growth Strategy

The company plans to engage in an aggressive marketing campaign targeted at signing new physicians in those areas where the company already has a large concentrations of physician customers.

The company intends to develop a series of new products that it can sell to its existing physician customers, and thereby squeeze more revenue out of each customer. We are targeting to increase per customer sales by 10% within 24 months.

The company also plans on continuing to develop its own technology so that its business processes are more efficient, with the result that our margins will increase. We believe we can achieve an improvement in gross margins of approximately 5% within twelve months.

We have been studying the competition and in particular those companies that compete with us in our major markets, such as California, New York and Florida. A number of those companies are privately held and we have approached some of them, and in confidential conversations found that we could be in a position to acquire 3 to 5 of them, increasing our revenues by 300%, provided we can raise the required capital.

PracticeXpert

There are several problems with it. First, there are too many words, and the print is too small, so people without their glasses, bad eyesight, or far away might not be able to read it. Second, the audience is going to be busy reading the slide, not listening to the speaker, and the impact of what the presenter is saying may well be lost. Third, with the entire speech written on the slide, the presenter may be inclined to read the slide, which will make the presentation boring. Now, look at that same slide crafted in a way to highlight just the most critical information.

With only these key highlights on the slide, the audience will quickly read the slide, understand the point the presenter is trying to make, and then will sit back to listen to the presenter as she expands on each point with the appropriate amount of detail.

Control the special effects. PowerPoint is a wonderful program. An expert user (talk to some college kids) can add in video, flash, sound effects, text that bounces in from all sides and angles, and a host of other special effects. If your company is in the entertainment business, or is a specialist in computer graphics, you might include a little extra, but for most companies, these special effects distract from the content of the presentation, and in some instances don't work properly. I was with one company when management presented to an investment fund, and halfway through the presentation, an audio recording was supposed to play. Well, it didn't play, and to make matters worse, the CEO of the company spent ten minutes of precious time fiddling with his computer trying to get the thing to play, while the fund manager sat across the conference room table fidgeting and looking at his watch. Leave the special effects out and focus on the content, not the flash.

Use pictures Wisely. I used to tell people to limit the use of pictures. My comment was: "Remember, this is a business presentation, not a report on your last vacation." However, I have changed my advice. The old saying that a picture is worth a thousand words is now truer than ever because people's attention spans are growing shorter and shorter, and many people simply can no longer read. That is not to say they cannot look at a page and identify the words. They might even be able to read the entire sentence, but increasingly people are losing the ability to comprehend a complex thought in written form. I know this for a fact. I have university students who not only cannot read the textbook but cannot understand written instructions on how to complete assignments and access information.

Choose pictured wisely and go for those pictures that have the most impact and relevance to the message you are trying to communicate. Pictures can send a powerful message if you have a product or facility that is hard to visualize, and if you end up giving your presentation in a place where you cannot bring samples of your product, but most people don't need a picture of a train or a plane if you say your market is transportation. Along with pictures, the use of graphs and charts can really bring your presentation alive. However, make sure you are not trying to cram too much data onto the slide. You don't want your audience to be spending all of their time trying to read the small print on a complex graph.

Below I have included five slides to make my point. These slides came from one of my former client's presentations.

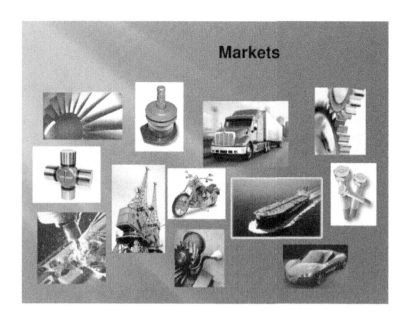

OK...there are a lot of pictures on this slide. So, who are their customers?

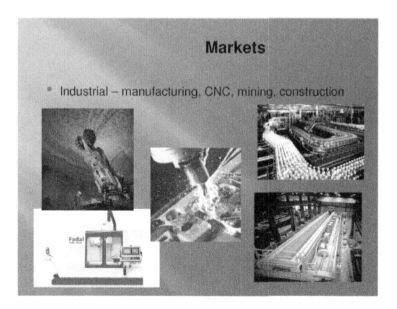

Ah-ha!! They have industrial customers.

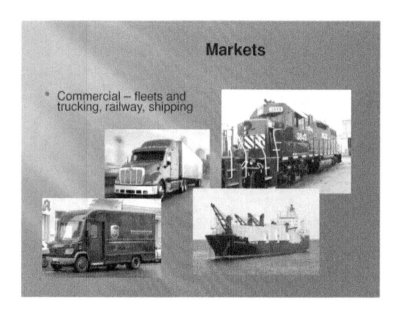

Oh...and they also have customers in the transportation business.

And some of those customers are international.

Look,…they also sell to retailers.

You would think from these five slides that this company was a billion-dollar corporation. In fact, this company actually had revenues of less than $1 million, and the bulk of its sales were not to any of the customers shown in these pictures, but most of their sales were to a handful of national and international distributors of industrial products.

One slide would have been far more effective; and while that slide was up on the screen, the CEO could then spend two or three minutes talking about its primary distributors, plans to expand its distribution base, major users of their products, and other important facts about the size of the markets and the universal demand for their products.

If you are going to use pictures, try to use pictures that evoke some sort of emotion. I remember seeing a presentation for a business idea that had something to do with pets. The CEO showed a slide of a mangy dog with patches of hair missing and a sad look on its face. He pointed at the picture and exclaimed, "Our product gets rid of that!" I can't remember the product, but I'll always remember that picture.

Tell a story. Even if you've never done any creative writing or written a screenplay, most people understand the concept of a storyline. The storyline is the sequence of events that lead us to the conclusion. You know—boy meets girl, boy loses girl, boy saves girl, boy gets the girl back. Think of most books or movies. Somehow, the central figure of the movie finds herself in a predicament. She avails herself of the information at hand, and based on a study of information available, makes a decision to take action (or not take action), and then the story concludes (usually favorably for the central figure, but not always).

Your PowerPoint needs to be presented with a similar sequence of events, only the sequence of events needs to lead to the conclusion that your company has a product for which there is a need, that the customers who need the product have the capacity to buy it, and that you as the manager can get the product to those customers who need it and have the capacity to buy it before your competitors do. You might be asking why you should prepare your presentation this way. The reason is simple. In a good PowerPoint presentation, the lights go on in the audience's mind before the presenter hits the punch line, just from the way the information is presented. The audience is following along, and suddenly they get it. Their eyes open wide; they see the potential. You've set the hook. It's the first step in getting a funding commitment for your company.

The plotline for your PowerPoint presentation is as follows:
- Title slide
- Introduction
- Company vision
- A brief history (very brief!!)
- Company today
- Market opportunity

- What is creating market demand
- Why current or competitive solutions don't work
- Bam! Company strategy
  (meet demand with solution)
- Company solution (its products)
- Product benefits (to the customer)
- Competitive advantages
- Strategy for growth
- Sale and marketing
- Projections
- Management
- Sources and uses of capital
- Business highlights.

If you have one slide for each of these bullet points, that's seventeen slides. That's too many!! We talked previously that the deck should be ten to twelve slides. That means you're going to have to cram more than one topic onto some slides. That's okay. Remember, the slides are guidelines for your presentation, and it is what you say in your presentation that counts, not what's on the slide. Obviously, you will need to tailor this outline slightly for your own business, but I would not venture far from the order I have listed here; in particular, don't change the order of that section of the presentation starting with the slide that I call "Market opportunity," and the slide labeled "Competitive advantages."

The exception to the ten to twelve slide rule is if you also decide to prepare a PowerPoint business plan that is meant to be read directly by a funding source without a speech or presentation. For PowerPoint business plans, you can increase the number of slides up to about 25 depending upon what information you need to tell the story. But I would not put in more than 25 as the likelihood of a reader reading each slide in detail is remote. Also, you need to make sure the written content is more than just bullet points, as without the elaboration of a presentation or speech, the message from each bullet point might not come across effectively.

Projections. Yes, you should have a slide in your presentation for financial projections. Like in your business plan, these projections should go out three to five years. However, these projections should be summary projections. Don't paste a copy of your Excel spreadsheet into PowerPoint and end up having something on the screen that is confusing and hard to read. You might give two projections, one with revenue and profit numbers, the other with some measure of business productivity (units sold, customers served, capacity utilized, etc.). If the funding source is interested beyond the presentation, you will send over your full financial package later, at which point the funding source will have the opportunity to study all your numbers and assumptions in detail.

Management. It is customary in a slide presentation to have a slide highlighting the management of the company. Companies tend to make two mistakes when talking about management (this includes board members or other advisors to the company). First, instead of a couple of key highlights on management's relevant experience, companies include management's entire bio or resume on the slide. Don't make the same mistake. All you need is a few keywords and relevant phrases. As an example:

Allan Smith, CEO – MBA, PhD., twenty years' experience in semiconductors, formerly CEO of Able Semiconductors and head of research for Quack Scientific.

In your business plan, you should include a bio or resume on each executive, but not in the PowerPoint. The second mistake is to "name drop" people who really are not involved in the business. I have seen PowerPoints that listed eight or ten supposedly influential people who were on the "Advisory Boards." And of course, in giving the presentation, the CEO named each one of these individuals and expounded on their major accomplishments. An example went something like this:

"Yes, Bob Davidson's on our Advisory Board. Bob's the former assistant commissioner of energy under Bush and was responsible for negotiating that new oil deal with OPEC."

In reality, Bob Davidson was the CEO's cousin's college roommate's dad, and as a favor, agreed to serve on the advisory board for a few shares, probably knows nothing about the business, and probably never was involved.

You'll get the point for having Davidson on your advisory board, but you'll lose points by yakking it up too much. Most advisory boards do little to help the business, and the higher their profile, the less they will probably do. We'll talk more about advisory boards and other influential people you may know later.

Use of funds. This is another one of those slides that you just must have. It's protocol. OK, you want to borrow $5 million, or you're looking for $10 million in equity capital, or whatever the case may be. You need to tell the funding source exactly how you are going to use the money. Of course, how you are going to use the money should tie into the rest of your presentation. Here's where you say:

"Remember on slide fifteen; we talked about doubling our production capacity to meet our growth objectives. Well, to do that, we need to acquire one more Guttenberg FDS 2000 for our plant, and that unit direct from the manufacturer in Bavaria costs $850,000."

The point here is that when you ask for capital, you need to know what you are going to use the money for. If it's a debt you're looking for, then you also need to have some idea of how fast you are going to pay it back. A final point...if you are looking for equity, and you are an early-stage enterprise, you need to tell the investor how the money will be used, how he or she will get the money back, and how much of a return he/she is going to get on the money (assuming the business unfolds according to plan). And remember, people who invest in high-risk, early-stage companies need a healthy return on their money (we'll talk more about this subject later too).

Investment Highlights

- Increasing demands as air fleets expected to double in 20 years
- Increasing demand for leases pushed by low cost carriers
- Uniquely positioned to leverage key industry relationships
- Limited competition due to barriers to entry
- Seasoned management with significant industry experience
- Above average returns fueled by low cost of operations

<u>Highlights.</u> The last slide in your presentation is the highlights or summary slide. This slide is important because it runs a common theme in your PowerPoint presentation, your pitch, and your two-pager snapshot. Basically, the highlight or summary slide is your last slide because it is the one that stays up on the screen while you field questions from the audience, and it is also the primary selling message of your deal. Your highlight slide needs to include key points that give the impression you will be successful, that demand exists for your product, that you are well-positioned to take advantage of that demand, that you will beat the pants off of the competition, and that everyone is going to make money or get paid back their loans with nice fat interest checks. Here is an example of a highlight slide for an aviation leasing company I did some work with a few years ago.

A final word about preparing your PowerPoint presentation... Just remember, your PowerPoint presentation and the speech you give that accompanies the presentation, is a replica of your business plan. Information that is given in your presentation, whether on a slide or orally, must be consistent with information written in your business plan document. You may not think of presenting your PowerPoint presentation as giving a speech; you might call it your oral presentation, what you say when the slides are up on the screen, or the talk that accompanies your PowerPoint. For the sake of brevity and consistency, we are going to call it your presentation speech, or just your speech.

<u>Summary of PowerPoint Presentation Dos and Don'ts</u>

- Keep it short—ten to twelve slides.

- Keep slide content to a minimum; use bullet points.
- Control special effects—the fewer, the better.
- Use pictures wisely.
- Tell a story.
- Include summary projections.
- Mention management <u>briefly.</u>
- Include a slide on the use of funds.
- End with the investment highlights.
- If you are doing a "Business Plan" PowerPoint, you can go up to 25 slides and use more text.

LET THE SHOW BEGIN

Now comes the second set of rules relating to your Power-Point presentation. These are the rules relating to your Power-Point speech. At this stage, you have prepared your business plan, prepared your two-pager, honed your pitch, and completed your PowerPoint presentation. Now it's time to present your story in front of an audience, whether it is an angel investor or your local banker or a team of investment banking professionals from Wall Street. This step in your fund-raising process is critical. Regardless of how good your business plan, your strategy, or your product, money guys put a lot of faith in the team that is driving the ship. From my experience, more funding opportunities are lost in this first critical meeting than anywhere else in the process. Do it well, and you get to the next step; do it poorly, and you're on to the next funding source. Here are the rules you need to follow to make your speech the most effective it can be.

Write it down. There are very few great orators in the world. The likes of John F. Kennedy and Martin Luther King, Jr. come along rarely, and in having seen presentations by hundreds of CEOs, I haven't seen any who even came close (a lot of them think they came close, but that's another story). Therefore, assuming you are not President Kennedy or Dr. King, you need to make sure you write down what you are going to say. Each slide in the presentation should have its own "talking points." These talking points are the information that the presenter is going to talk about, while the slide is on the screen. There are several ways of writing down these talking points. PowerPoint has a notes section for each slide, and you could put the notes of what you want to say on each slide and then print it out as a guide. Alternatively, you could put it on a Word document with a separate page labeled for each slide, or you could use a card system. Whatever works for you, do it. Then use a printed copy of these talking points as you give the presentation. Referring to the talking points, as opposed to referring to the slide, gives you two advantages. First, by reviewing the talking points, you will make sure you cover all the important information you want to say, relating to each slide. Second, by talking from your talking points, when the talking points for that slide are finished, you will naturally move on to the next slide. This keeps you from talking about information on the coming slides before those slides go up on the screen. I have seen CEOs put up their first slide, talk for fifteen minutes, and then finally realize they have not been advancing the slides, so when they do advance the slides, all of the material has been covered, and they are left saying, "Oh, well we talked about that already." Now the CEO looks foolish and unprepared.

Some presenters opt to put their talking points on their cell phones. That works, but I have also seen presenters who accidentally hit something on their phone, and they are busy searching trying to get the right screen back up. Younger people who are comfortable with their phones might use this technique. Obviously, you should adopt a technique that will work best for you.

Practice. To give an effective speech, you need to practice. One thing to be looking for is that you are talking about the slide that is on the screen, when it is on the screen. A second thing to look for is the time. We used to get twenty-five minutes for a presentation. Today, you'll probably want to trim that back to fifteen minutes. Attention spans are not what they used to be, and my experience is that listeners stop listening if the presentation is too long. Depending upon the audience, you may begin to lose them in the first five minutes.

When you practice, if possible, practice in front of a critical audience. Get feedback from people who listen to your speech and how it was presented—what was effective and what was not effective. Pay attention to your tone of voice (just like a Sunday morning preacher, this is your opportunity to bore your audience to tears or get them jumping up and down in their seats). Find out if you are using words that are too technical or are filling your speech with buzzwords. No one is impressed by that, particularly not the money guys. You don't have to have an on-stage presence like a *60 Minutes* interviewer, but you can significantly increase the message you are trying to deliver by putting enthusiasm and simplicity into your speech.

Don't read the slides. We covered this topic a little when we discussed preparing your presentation. Remember when we talked about not putting too much information on the slide? You don't want the slide to be an essay. It should contain a few well-crafted bullet points. Remember, the slide is not the presentation. The presentation is all of those talking points that you have written down, and that you have practiced. The slide is a guide to your presentation and reinforces the points you are trying to make.

I have seen many presentations where the presenter simply read what was on the slide—no embellishment, no added details, no further explanation. In such cases, I am usually wondering why we even need the presenter. Just give me the PowerPoint presentation, and I'll read it myself. Remember, if we are not presenting and we just want someone to read the PowerPoint, then we send them the business plan version of the PowerPoint.

Look at the audience. It doesn't matter if you are giving

your presentation to a banker in his office across his desk, or if you are presenting at a conference to hundreds of Wall Street mucky-mucks. Your focus and attention should be on the person or people listening to you. You should be looking at them in the eye as often as possible. There are several reasons why. First, let's look at what happens when you don't look at the audience. Typically, presenters who don't look at the audience are looking at one of two places—at their notes or at the computer or projection screen. If you're constantly looking at your notes, you're probably reading them, or you're unprepared. This comes through in your presentation and, remember, the guys who have the money are evaluating you as much as they are evaluating your business or your products. You should practice your speech enough times so that you only need a very quick glance at your notes between each slide. **Also, eye contact with the money guys is very important; making eye contact builds trust, and trust is a key element of getting money.** People who don't look you straight in the eye seem shifty or disinterested as if their mind is somewhere else.

An even greater presentation sin than not looking at your audience is staring at the screen. I have seen CEOs of billion-dollar corporations get up in front of a room full of Wall Street investment bankers and analysts and spend the entire time with their back to the audience while they look at, and talk to, the screen. Even worse, is when the presenter is standing at a podium with a microphone, and every time he turns his head to look at the screen behind him, his voice fades out because he moves his mouth away from the microphone. I have seen these types of things happen so often that it amazes me that these clowns can raise any money at all, let alone run big corporations. The audience's job is to look at the computer screen; your job is to look at your audience, large or small, as often as you can. A glance at the screen, while you are not talking, to make sure you have the right slide up, is OK, but once you've confirmed it's the right slide, look at the person/people you're giving the presentation to, and then start to speak.

Using a microphone. Professional broadcasters, singers, and speakers know how to use a microphone. Most of the rest of us don't. So, you need to learn how to use it. First, you need to get close. Have a look at a singer and see how close that singer holds the microphone to his or her mouth. Most of the time, it is close enough that the singer could lick it (although I wouldn't recommend doing so). If it is a stationary microphone at a podium, staying close to the mic is not so difficult. However, if it is a handheld mic, it is not so easy. People tend to use their hands and arms for gestures. Too often, I have seen a speaker swing his arm away from his body for emphasis, only to have the microphone not pick up what he said because it was too far away from his mouth. A good trick is to hold your elbow tight against your body. In this way, the microphone is more likely to stay close to your face.

Hard copies and technical difficulties. These two topics go hand in hand. You should always have hard copies of your PowerPoint presentation available. However, don't hand out copies of your presentation before you give the presentation. If you do, your audience will not be listening to your speech, they will be glancing through your presentation, and while you are talking about slide four, they will be reading slide sixteen, and much of your message may be lost. Keep the hard copies in your briefcase and hand them out, along with any other material you want the money guys to have at the end of the presentation.

The only two exceptions are when someone specifically asks for a copy in advance, or when you find yourself having to give your PowerPoint presentation without your computer. Yes, it can happen. Computers crash, files get corrupted, projectors don't work—there can be a host of reasons why you may not be able to give your presentation from your computer. It may be you thought the meeting was going to happen in a conference room, but the money guys decided to go for lunch. There is nothing as foolish as a CEO trying to balance his laptop on the lunch table between the Cobb salad and the fish of the day, trying to give his PowerPoint presentation. In any of these instances, when using PowerPoint is not a viable option, whip out your hard copies, put the computer away, and give your speech using paper instead of a screen.

Today with cell phones you can also have your presentation on your cell phone, and for some reason, if your laptop breaks down or the projector does not work, you can email or text your presentation from your cell phone to your audience (assuming the audience is not too large). It is also possible to store your presentation on some shared space in the cloud, such as Google Docs, and you can share the link with your audience.

Fielding questions. In any presentation, there are going to be questions. Presentations work best if the questions come toward the end of the presentation. There are two ways of handling questions. One is to request that the audience let you complete your presentation, and then you will field questions. The second way is to take questions as you go along. I recommend you ask people to keep their questions until the end, because questions can often interrupt the presenter and throw the presentation off track, and also many questions early on in a presentation will get answered later in the presentation as the presentation runs its course.

However, if you decide to take questions as you go along, you should have a strategy in place for those questions. My recommendation is that if the question specifically relates to the topic at hand, answer it. If it doesn't, defer the question until later. As an example, assume you are talking about your current customer base, and you have a slide up that says:

-    60 percent of sales to big-box retailers

Now, someone in the audience asks, "Is the Home Depot one of your customers?" By all means, answer the question. This question clearly relates to the slide on the screen. The Home Depot is a big-box retailer. Someone else in the audience asks, "Is your factory AS9000 certified?" Don't answer the question, even if the answer is simple. AS9000 certification has nothing to do with your big-box retailer customers, and changing the topic from your customer base to your factory disrupts the continuity of your presentation. Your response should be, "Good question...hang onto it and bring it up again when we talk about production and our manufacturing facilities."

Three characters will occasionally rear their heads and make your presentation more difficult. The first one is the "Wall Street Kid." The Wall Street kid is out to make a name for himself, and he is working on fifty deals at a time. He is twenty minutes late for what you thought was going to be an hour-long meeting, and he tells you when he arrives that he has another meeting scheduled in twenty minutes. You promptly begin to give your presentation, and instead of sitting back and listening, the Wall Street Kid is firing dozens of unrelated questions at you. When this happens, pause, close your computer, and say, "It seems to me this meeting would be more effective if I just answer your questions as opposed to giving my formal presentation, and any that I cannot answer right now, I'll write down and send you an email response in the next day or two." I have seen seasoned executives, harried looks on their faces, flipping from front to back in their presentation, trying to find the slide that answers these random questions. They look foolish and unprepared, and waste even more of the little time they have with the Wall Street Kid. Just remember, no matter how obnoxious he seems, he isn't called the Wall Street kid for nothing.

The second guy to watch out for is the "Questionator." The Questionator will have a million questions for you, 90 percent of which are completely irrelevant to the discussion, or to make a funding decision. The reason the Questionator is a problem is that answering his questions takes you away from the time you could be spending telling the money guys all the great reasons for putting money into your deal. Remember, time is precious, and every minute you have should be a minute of selling or a minute of learning.

Let's say you made the decision to outsource your call center to India. Your call center operations account for approximately 5 percent of your total costs, so while they are significant, they are not the major portion of your expenses. The Questionator will immediately ask, "Are your outsourced operations in Bangalore or Chennai." Of course, it makes absolutely no difference if your outsourced operations are in Bangalore or Chennai. Now you are forced to answer the question. Maybe you don't know, and if you say you don't know, The Questionator will look at you with a look of disdain, and then he will ask some other equally useless question. If you say Bangalore, then he will ask, "Why not Chennai?" And if you say Chennai, he will ask, "Why not Bangalore?" Then if you say you chose Chennai as opposed to Bangalore because the company you are dealing with is in Chennai, he will say, "Why don't you look at some of the companies in Bangalore?" as if you have nothing better to do. It is impossible to answer any of his questions to his satisfaction, and I have seen meetings that lasted an hour where forty minutes were taken up by the Questionator asking useless questions. That's forty minutes of time when you could have been convincing the money guys to put money into your deal. There is only one way to deal with the Questionator. Tell him as politely as possible that while you would like to answer every question he has, and are happy to do so, you really want to cover your presentation, but too many questions make you lose your continuity and train of thought. If he continues to monopolize the question period, then simply say, "If you don't mind, I'd like to table your question to make sure I have a chance to answer the questions some of the other folks in the room might have."

The third guy to watch out for in presentations is "I'm The Man." I'm The Man is almost as bad as the Questionator. He may ask some relevant questions, but the question is always posed as an opportunity for him to show you, and the rest of the people, how "in the know" and "connected" he is.

Let's say your company is a manufacturer of pet supplies. When you begin talking about competition, I'm The Man asks, "Ever hear of Doggy Delights out of Seattle?"

You think for a second, then respond, "Yes, I have. I met the owner at one of the pet industry conventions a few years ago. I can't remember his name."

Now you've just opened the door for I'm The Man. He says, taking another gulp of his coffee for effect, "Yup. That would be Sam Levinson. Good ole' Sam. Back in '97 when I was with Richardson Peabody, we raised old Sam $25 million from Union Investment Funds, so he could buy out those two companies down in Texas." He turns to one of his compatriots at the table. "Hey, George...do you remember that deal? Ha...got it done by the skin of our teeth...." And then "I'm The Man" spends five or more minutes of your valuable time reminiscing and name dropping. As for Doggy Delights, they sell dog treats, and you sell bird cages, so they are not a competitor; they make products for a completely different segment of the market, so any discussion of them is meaningless. The worst thing is, I'm The Man will use this same tactic to commandeer the conversation a dozen times while you are trying to tell your story. There is no easy solution for I'm The Man, but the two tactics you can use are to claim ignorance about the person, company, or incident he is talking about (otherwise he will draw you into a lengthy discussion about the said topic) or to politely suggest that you have a high level of interest in his "insightful" and "in the know" knowledge and maybe you can have a private meeting after the main one is finished to discuss.

Fielding questions, part two. Now that you know how to deal with the Wall Street Kid, the Questionator, and I'm The Man, we need to discuss how you answer questions in general. Second only to giving a poor presentation, doing a poor job of answering questions is the next greatest deal killer. Questions are the way the money guys get sold on the deal. Good answers to questions confirm to the money guys that you know what you're talking about, that you understand your market and competition, that you understand the risks associated with your business, and that you know how to execute. Later, we will discuss certain specific questions, and how to answer them, but here we are going to discuss the general rules for answering questions. These rules are very simple, but you would be surprised at how poorly many CEOs answer questions.

I am amazed at the number of times that I have heard a CEO give the wrong answer to a question. Either they don't listen to the question, or they misunderstand the question. So, rule number one is "understand the question." Some questions are poorly asked, so it might be easy to misunderstand what the questioner is getting at. If there is any doubt whatsoever, confirm with the person who asked the question exactly what the question is. Here's an example:

MG: "Dave, what's your selling cycle like?"

Now, I would think this question relates to the "sales cycle," commonly known as the length of time it takes between the first contact with a customer and the customer's decision to purchase. However, it's possible this question is directed at something else.

CEO: "Let me make sure I understand your question. Are you asking about the time it takes for a customer to make the decision to purchase our products, or are you referring to the seasonality of our business?"

MG: "Well, I was actually referring to your sales cycle on an annual basis. It seems like you probably sell a lot more in the summer, and then you would in the winter."

In this case, if the CEO had gone on about how long it took to sell a customer, he would not have answered the question.

Once you understand the question, answer the question. Rule number two is to be "brief and to the point." If your answer isn't detailed enough, the person asking the question can always ask follow-up questions. But if you are long-winded and cover a lot of ground that the question was not intended to cover, you will suffer three consequences. First, you will be perceived as being long-winded, and long-winded people are thought of as being poor listeners, poor communicators, and poor managers. Second, you may get bogged down in irrelevant details that sidetrack the conversation, or worse, bring up facts and circumstances that make the company look bad. Third, you may waste valuable time that can be better spent selling the money guys on your deal. I had one experience with a medical technology company CEO at a meeting with an investment banker in New York. This company had gone public several years ago. At the meeting, one of the money guys asked the CEO, "When did you go public?" The answer was something like March 1997. However, the CEO began talking, and spent ten minutes giving all of the details of how an early investor in the company had recommended they go public, how that investor had introduced him to a deal guy that did reverse mergers, how they had gone through the process of finding a shell, and on and on and on!!! It was way too much information and a total waste of time when we could have been selling the money guy on the deal instead. I stress this point so much because, unfortunately, the people who answer questions this way—by talking for too long and giving too much information—for the most part, don't realize they are doing it. They think they are being thorough. So, this is one of those areas where you need to ask someone who will tell you the truth about how you do in answering questions.

A special word of advice for those of you with technical backgrounds...this is a trap most often committed by CEOs with technical backgrounds who think that an answer to a question, to be complete, must include every contingency and variable. If you are a NASA scientist guiding a crew of astronauts to the moon, maybe you need to answer questions in this matter. If you are in front of the money guys, you don't. And if you do, you may very quickly lose your audience. In fact, by keeping your questions brief, it is more conversational, with more opportunity for back-and-forth engagement. But if you give long-winded technical answers, chances are the money guys will tune you out, and will be playing with their cell phones, texting, answering emails, making to-do lists, or thinking about some other deal they are working on.

This rule is so important that I will give another example. I worked with a gentleman who was trying to raise money for an alcohol beverage company. He had developed a promising product and needed capital to get production off the ground. The problem was this gentleman had launched the product previously, and for many reasons, his company had to shut down. He had placed this product into a new company and was trying to relaunch it. The new company had nothing to do with the old company. There was no reason to mention the old company. The product had only been on the market a short while when the previous company closed. The story of the old company was irrelevant. However, in meetings with money guys, this gentleman insisted on telling the story about how the product had been launched previously, had done exceedingly well, but in the end, his company had to shut down. He didn't just glance over this topic; he spent a lot of time giving all of the details. The instant he did that, I could see the money guys start to lose interest. Instead of getting excited about this product and the new company, they were concerned about my client's management experience and if he could run the new company. Of course, this generated many questions, and the focus of each meeting became more of a discussion about the company that went out of business, as opposed to the new opportunity. Needless to say, my client never raised the money for this deal.

The third rule is to "be honest." Most CEOs don't like being put on the spot. In fact, they often specialize in putting other people on the spot. They are the ones with the riveting questions for employees and suppliers. So, when a question comes around that is tough to answer, some CEOs fall into the trap of fabricating answers or embellishing assumptions into facts. Doing so will come back to bite you. If you don't know the answer to some question, say so. If the answer is important, make a note of it and get back to the questioner after the meeting with the answer. If you felt foolish because you couldn't answer the question, then use it as a learning experience, find the answer, and make sure you don't make the same mistake again.

The fourth rule is to "remember the difference between facts and opinions." Facts can be supported by evidence. Opinions may be correct, but typically are based on a person's perspective or experience and may not actually be correct at all. The area in which I see CEOs make this mistake repeatedly is assessing customers, competitors, and markets. You may believe from conversations with a handful of customers that physicians are looking to automate their offices, but that is substantially different from having, in hand, a survey of 5,000 physicians in which 90 percent said they intended to automate office processes. When possible, try to use facts to support the answers to your questions, as opposed to opinions; and when you do use opinions, make it clear on what you based your opinion.

The final rule is "to make sure you've answered the question." When you finish answering each question, you should ask, "Is that what you were looking for?" or "Did I answer your question?" Doing so shows a great sign of professionalism on your part and makes sure that the person asking the question got his or her question answered.

Follow up. We'll talk more about follow up in a general sense later on, but specifically, as it relates to your presentation, there are some things you need to do. Get the name, email address, and, if possible, the business card of everyone at the meeting. Make sure you send an email thanking each person for his or her time. Make sure you deliver the answers to any unanswered questions, and that you deliver any additional requested material on a timely basis. This step is extremely important. I worked with a client that had a meeting with a funding source that was very interested. That funding source asked for some additional information. This is information that might have taken my client two hours to prepare. Three weeks later, my client delivered the requested information. The funding source was no longer interested, and specifically cited my client's late response as the primary reason.

Finally, ask the money guys about next steps and when you can expect to hear back from them. It's your job to ensure you follow up. Even if they are interested, these guys see many, many deals, and after a while, one deal starts to flow into the next, and like most of us, we work on the squeaky wheel. Find out when you can expect to hear back, and if you don't, call them.

<u>Summary of Presenting Dos and Don'ts</u>

- Write down what you plan to say.
- Practice giving your presentation.
- Don't read the slides.
- Look at the audience; make eye contact.
- Keep hard copies handy, but don't give them out before your presentation unless you have to.
- Be prepared to give you a presentation without the computer in case of technical difficulties.
- Field questions properly.
- Watch out for Wall Street Kid.
- Watch out for the Questionator.
- Watch out for I'm The Man.
- Answer the questions.
- Keep answers brief.
- Be honest.
- Remember the difference between facts and opinions.
- Follow up with people you meet with.

A RARE FIND

Somewhere in your journey to raise capital, someone is going to ask you this question, "What other businesses are like your business?" I've lost count of the number of times I've heard a business owner answer that question with "we're unique" or "there are no other businesses like ours." Wrong!! Your business is not unique. There are hundreds of businesses like yours out there. And you know what? That's OK. In fact, that's great, because it means you will have an easier time raising money.

I know what you're saying. You're saying, "Mike, you're wrong. My business really is unique. I did a search on the Internet, and I am the only company in the United States of America that takes a recording of your dog's bark while he is alive, and then when he dies, I take your dog, stuff him, put a machine inside of him with a playback device and a motion detector, and every time you walk by, your dead dog barks at you."

OK, let me explain. I am going to tell you about a business, and I want you to tell me what kind of business it is. This business comes up with a concept based on what they see as current trends and market conditions. Based on the concept, they develop a budget and get the capital for the business—usually a lot of capital. They put their creative people to work and enter a phase of planning and design that could take years. When the planning and designing phase is complete, they then begin to make the product. This product takes a long time to finish, usually years, and by the time the product is finished and ready to sell to the public, the company runs the risks that people's tastes may have changed, or the market may have changed, and they may not be able to sell it to the public and make a profit on their investment.

Reread the above paragraph. Venture a guess? I expect that if I handed this paragraph to someone working for Universal Studios, he or she would tell me it is obviously a feature film production company. If I gave this to someone who works for Donald Trump, he or she would immediately tell me it's a real estate development company. Surprisingly the two businesses have a great many similarities, with perhaps the one differentiator—the finished product in the movie business can be shown around the globe, while a real estate development is stuck in one location.

The point is that many businesses are very similar. They are not as unique as you might think. But that is a good thing, because money guys don't understand unique and don't want unique. Money guys look for patterns. Is your business model like a real estate developer, or like a fast-food chain? Is it like a clothing designer or a muffler shop? I've never actually sat down and counted them (probably some academic in some university has), but there are a finite number of business models. So, what you want to do is find a readily understandable business model that you can compare yourself to, and of course, you want to compare yourself in a favorable way. Then when you get asked that question by some money guy, he will be impressed that you understand the fundamentals of how your business works. And this is something you should be able to do, no matter how big or how small your business is. I should tell you that sometimes it's not easy. It's not easy, not because there are no businesses like yours; it's not easy because you haven't thought enough about the essence of your business. I suggest you try to think of your business, not in terms of its product, but in terms of what your business delivers to your customers. Is the foundation of your business built on convenience, predictability, cost, features, regulation, reputation, or something else? Why do your customers (or your expected customers) want to do business with you? If you begin to answer these questions, then you can begin to build the statement of what kind of businesses you are like. Here are a couple of examples:

"Although we only have one location, we are kind of like McDonald's. We have a limited product selection, very reasonable prices, our customers are repeat customers, we have a very convenient location, and we deliver a very consistent level of product quality, with every customer experience. That's also why we think our planned expansion will be successful."

"We're kind of like a custom home builder, and only we do it with motorcycles. A custom homebuilder builds the home the way the customer wants it, including materials, fixtures, and features. And the custom homebuilder makes more profit than a builder of tract homes, per unit. We do the same with motorcycles. Every unit is custom built to a customer's specifications, and our profit per bike is triple the industry average."

"My new auto repair shop will be very similar to a chain down in Florida. They, too, provide a large lounge with televisions, the Internet, books, latte machines, computers, and other things for customers to keep busy while they wait for their car. And if you read the latest copy of Entrepreneur, that company is growing at the rate of 200 percent per year. We don't have a repair shop like that in Grand Rapids, but if it's working in Florida, it should work just as well here."

Those are just a few examples, but I am sure you get the idea. When you say to me, "McDonald's," I have a mental picture of what that represents and understand how the application of that business model will be successful. Similarly, when you say custom homebuilder, that gives me an image, and I quickly understand how building anything else to customer specs, as opposed to a production run, should drive increased profits. If you can point to another company that is doing the same thing you want to do, only in a different geographical region, I can make a better decision as to your chances of success. As a result, if I were one of the money guys looking to fund your business, I would have a higher comfort level knowing that other businesses that are similar to yours (although perhaps in different industries, or perhaps in the same industry but in a different geographical location) have achieved success.

READY FOR A FIGHT

This chapter is about handling suggestions or criticisms about your business or your plans. If there is one common trait amongst most money guys, whether traditional bankers, hard moneylenders, investment bankers, or fund managers, they all think they could do a better job of running your business than you. In some cases, they are probably right (and we'll talk more about that later). I would venture to bet that, in most cases, they are wrong. I know several money guys who made the decision to join a company, or start a company, only to be back on the money side of things a year later. Same goes for attorneys and accountants. It's much easier to sit on the outside and second-guess what the management team is doing, kind of, like we all do when we watch the Super Bowl.

There are many reasons why they think this way. First, most of them have a business education, and MBAs think they know everything (I should know, I have an MBA, and when I discovered I didn't know everything, I decided to go back to school). Second, they have probably provided money to companies that failed, and probably felt they know why those companies failed, and what those companies could have done differently to succeed. Third, they have probably looked at a lot of businesses in trouble that were looking for money. In that process, they were able to diagnose the problems that got those companies into hot water. Finally, they have met with the owners of hundreds if not thousands of executive teams, toured hundreds if not thousands of shops, factories, and offices, and read hundreds if not thousands of business plans. If you look at it this way, you must give them some credit for knowledge.

But by the same token, many of these money guys think it is part of their job to try to tell you how to run your business. That can be a problem. Most CEOs, whether they are the head of a fledgling enterprise or the head of a large corporation, don't like to be told what to do. In fact, many are downright unreceptive to advice from anyone on how to do anything. This, too, is understandable. It's tough to be the head of a company. And to get there, most CEOs have had to fight the naysayers, the doubters, the dooms-dayers, and all of the other people that are all too ready to tell the CEO that it's too difficult, it's too risky, it won't work, it's never been done, and a load of other less than encouraging comments. So, when faced with someone who tries to steer the CEO in a different direction, the hair on the back of the CEO's neck rises, the claws and fangs come out, and the CEO gets ready to battle anyone who suggests that his/her vision of reality is not completely and entirely correct and accurate.

Why are we talking about this? Why is this important for raising money? **Because one of the golden rules of raising capital is never to argue with the money guys**—never, never, never. Why? Because money guys don't like to be told their ideas won't work, are stupid, or can't be done...and they have the money! And remember, they think they could run your business better than you do. I can hear what you are saying to yourself. "Aren't they making their loan or investment decision based upon my business plan, my projections, and my security?" Yes, they are—in part. But there are a whole lot of other factors that influence decision-making (we'll talk more about this later, too). One of them is their assessment of your ability to take constructive criticism and helpful suggestions when things go wrong. And if you argue with the money guys, you've just proven to them that you are not open to constructive criticism and helpful suggestions, and that if things don't go as planned, you're going to be difficult to deal with.

OK, if you can never argue with the money guys, what should you do if there is a problem? That depends. There are two situations that happen with money guys. The first one is the probing question. It is not usually a "how" question; it is usually a "why" question. Let's look at a typical conversation between a money guy and the CEO of a company.

MG: "Bob, with your software, you must get a lot of inbound customer calls with installation issues, warranty claims, and maintenance. How do you handle your call center?"

CEO: "We decided to put our call center in Oklahoma City."

Next comes the "why" question. The problem is that it could be a legitimate why question, in that the money guy really wants to know what was behind your decision to locate your call center in Oklahoma City, or he could be asking it because he thinks you should have located it somewhere else, and is itching at the opportunity to dispute your logic and demonstrate how smart a businessman he really is. Here comes his question.

MG: "Oklahoma City? Why not India? That's what everyone seems to be doing these days."

Now you have a problem. Do you defend Oklahoma City? If you don't, then it looks like you made a decision without doing a lot of research. That's not good, and you will lose points with the money guys. But if you do, and this guy is married to Indian outsourcing, he is going to think you're a schmuck for not outsourcing your call center to India. Let's look at both of those scenarios.

CEO: "We actually did a lot of analysis before making the decision. We ran the numbers up and down, and Oklahoma just makes more sense. It's centrally located in the middle of the country, everyone already speaks English with no accent, the wage rates are some of the lowest in the country, facilities costs are low, and the workforce tends to be very stable. We did look at India, but we had problems with their English; the ten companies we talked to all had high turnover; and while the direct labor costs were lower than Oklahoma City, by the time we factored in seven or eight trips a year to India, we just think we're getting a far better service level for our customers at home."

Now, if the money guy were asking a legitimate question, you would get this response.

MG: "That sounds reasonable. I am really interested in what companies are doing about call centers because I hear mixed things about India. Maybe it's right for some companies and not others. Interesting...."

However, if he was not asking a legitimate question, you might get this response.

MG: "You know, Bob, you might want to rethink that decision. We've raised $50 million for Indian outsourcing companies in the past six months, and our analysts are telling us that's where it's at. Any company that continues to do its outsourcing domestically is going to get eaten alive."

Oh, oh...now your chances of getting funded have just dropped by about 50 percent. So, what should you have done? You should have tested the waters with the money guy to see where he was going with his "why" question. You should have responded this way.

CEO: "You know, India was at the top of our list, and it was a tough decision, and the one that's not too late to change. How do you think we should handle the call center issue?"

By the way the money guy answers, you will know if he is trying to tell you how to run your business, or if he is just on a fact-finding mission. Let's say it's the latter.

MG: "Bob, we just backed this Indian outsourcing company, and it's really clear. Anyone who has a domestic call center is going to get eaten alive."

Now you can play right into his hands with your response. Again, remember, you don't want to argue with the money guys. Even if you have run the numbers six ways to Sunday, and the very best business decision would be Oklahoma City, you simply cannot tell the money guy he is wrong. You need to downplay the issue and demonstrate your flexibility and eagerness to adopt new solutions. You should say something like this.

CEO: "You know, Tom, what we really need is an expert at this Indian outsourcing stuff who can really help us set it up properly. Sounds like you've got just the right connection with that company you funded. Once we get this next round of financing in place, I'm counting on you to make an introduction."

Now you've just increased your chances of getting funded by 50 percent. Not only have you stroked the money guy's ego, he thinks that you're a really reasonable guy, and he's also thinking about the commission he's going to get from the Indian company when he introduces you to them. If you never get the money from this money guy, nothing is lost. But if you do, he'll probably forget to make the introduction; and even if he does, you can go through the motions, have a few meetings to be polite, and then come up with a dozen excuses why you can't make the change. Remember, be very wary of the "why" questions, as they often come from someone with a bias as to how that question should be answered. If you don't answer the question the way the person asking the question thinks you should, you've lost points and lessened your chances of getting funding.

The second situation usually occurs at the end of the meeting. A lot of money guys think it's their duty to leave you with some pearls of wisdom. After you've finished your presentation and all questions have been answered, the money guy will say something like this.

MG: "Bob, great presentation. We're really interested in your business, and I'm going to have our analyst dig a little deeper. We might be able to do something."

Now you're excited. This looks really promising. The analyst is going to call you, and maybe there's a chance. Then the money guy continues.

MG: "You know, Bob, in that product roll-out, I think you're making a big mistake by not doing an infomercial. That's one of the best ways to launch a product these days, particularly one like yours. I'd really consider that if I were you."

Now what money guy doesn't know is that your college roommate runs one of the most successful infomercial companies in the country, and you've already spent a day with the infomercial experts. Based on your product complexity and cost structure you were told the numbers just don't work. Your product just doesn't have the characteristics of a good infomercial product. So, what do you say? Remember the rule; never argue with the money guys. "But hang on Mike," I can hear you saying. "I'm not arguing. I'm just going to tell him that we've already discussed that route and rejected it." That's arguing!!! **Even if you're right and the money guy is dead wrong, it's still arguing!!** This is what you should say.

CEO: "You know, we did look at the possibility of doing an infomercial a while back, but based on what you say, we need to have another look at it. That might really jump-start our sales."

Remember, if you don't get funded, it doesn't make any difference. But if you start to argue with a money guy now, you'll probably never get funded by him, and if you do get funded, no big deal. Once you have the money, you can usually run the business your way. If the subject ever comes up again, you can tell the money guy all the sordid details about the info-mercial company and even send him a copy of the product rejection letter.

This golden rule is so important I am going to repeat it again. **Never, never, never argue with the money guys.** And to go even further, any idea or suggestion they have should be treated as brilliant. Write it down, tell them you'll look into it, and see if you can change your plan to include their wonderful idea.

As the final part of this chapter, I am going to tell you a story about funding with which I was involved. I was working with a company and had found a private equity fund that was interested in the company and was willing to invest $6 million in it. Due diligence was complete, documents were drawn up, and we all gathered in a conference room to sign the documents. The CEO was a curmudgeon in his early sixties. The fund manager was a hotshot MBA in his early thirties. During the document signing, in a casual conversation, the fund manager made a suggestion to the CEO. The suggestion was heartily rejected, with a comment akin to "I've been in this business for thirty years, and it just doesn't work that way." Now, for all I know, that could be a verifiably true statement. However, the fund manager suddenly found some problem with the documents and said he needed to contact the attorney to correct them. We were told the documents would be corrected, and we would reconvene the next day to finish the signing. An hour later, I received a call from the fund manager stating they had changed their mind and would not be funding the deal.

Let me say it again. **<u>Never, never, never argue with the money guys!</u>**

WHAT COMPETITION?

    This chapter deals with something similar to the chapter on being unique. It relates to competition. Sooner or later, the money guys are going to ask, "Who are your competitors?" The most foolish thing out of the mouth of any business owner or CEO is, "We don't have competition." It's foolish for two reasons. First, it's most likely not true. Second, even if it is true, no money guy is going to believe it.

    First, let's talk about competition and then we'll talk about how to answer this question. Every business has competition, and it comes in many forms. Let's take the example of two hamburger restaurants across the street from each other. This scene is something you will see at thousands of intersections across the country. On one corner is McDonald's, and on the other corner is Burger King. Clearly, these two stores are competitors. Now, what if only one of these stores, let's says the Burger King, was the only hamburger store in town. Would it have no competition? Of course, it would have competition. While there may not be any other burger restaurants in the town, what about another fast food restaurant, like KFC. Would that be competition? Of course, customers could make a choice to eat chicken or burgers. Now, what if there were no other fast-food restaurants in town, but there was a Morton's. Would that be competition? Absolutely, because customers could make a choice between a cheap meal and an expensive one. What if there were no other restaurants in this town, but there was a grocery store. Would that be competition? Of course, it would because customers could decide to eat out or eat at home. Now, what if there were no other restaurants in town or grocery stores, but there was a garden supply center. Could that be competition? Yes, because customers could decide to grow their own food or go out to eat. What about the local gas station? Is that competition? Yes, because customers could decide to eat or to put gas in their car.

I think I've taken this example far enough (maybe too far), but the point is that there is plenty of competition for every product. That is simply because we have a limited supply of money (at least most of us do), but an almost unlimited supply of things upon which we can spend that money. Therefore, to suggest that there is no competition is ludicrous.

So how then should you answer the question about the competition? First, you should acknowledge that there is some competition. Then you should be able to identify who or what that competition is. Let's face it; if someone is going to spend money on your product, by its very nature, it implies that a customer is not going to spend his or her money on some other product (assuming a customer spends all of his money, which most consumers and businesses in the U.S. do, including the Government—in fact, most spend more money than they have). Then once you have identified who the competition is, you should be able to explain why a customer would do business with you rather than with the competition.

This is an extremely useful exercise because the reasons why a customer will spend money on your product, as opposed to the competition, are part of your competitive advantage. You are offering something that the customer can either not get elsewhere, or the way you offer it is more appealing than the way other businesses offer that same product. That appeal may be price, location, convenience, service level, or more. Whatever it is, it is very important to the future earning potential of your business. Once you have identified what your competitive advantage is, then you can talk intelligently about your competition. But take the time to really understand what your competitive advantage is, and why customers do business with you (or why you think they will do business with you). A lot of businesses get this wrong. I think for years, airlines thought the meals on flights made a difference, only to realize that most travelers could give a hoot about the food. Travelers are more interested in price, convenient flight times, and on-time take-off. Sometimes, on the other hand, it's really obvious. I was in a small town in Michigan a while back. I had gotten in late and went to the local restaurant for a bite to eat. It was packed. I casually commented to another patron, "Food must be good. Look at the crowd." She looked at me strangely and said, "Food's not that good at all…, but it's five past midnight, and this is the only restaurant that's open for forty miles."

OK, so now you know what your competitive advantage is—why customers buy from you, instead of from the competition. Now you're ready to talk about your competitors. So, when one of the money guys asks who your competitors are, have a couple of handy phrases ready.

"Yes, there are two other tires stores in town. But they both close on Sunday and at 6:00 every evening. I'm open until midnight every day, and on Sundays, and in those hours, we do 40 percent of our business."

"Yes, we are right across the street from Burger King. And Burger King does a good business, but this is a small town, and everyone in town knows our burgers just taste a whole lot better. That's why they keep coming back—for fifteen years now. Ask anyone in town you meet, and they'll tell you as much."

"Our board game is brand new, and there is no other similar board game on the market right now…that we're aware of.

However, based on our surveys, we believe customers who buy games will buy our game, rather than some of the games currently on the market, because of these four specific features...."

Hopefully, by now, you're getting the picture. You do have competition, you do need to acknowledge that competition, and you especially need to know and understand, from the customer's perspective, why that customer would choose to do business with you, rather than with your competitors.

TILL DEATH DO
US PART

I've heard a hundred CEOs utter this line: "I've been trying to raise money for a year. I've had lots of serious interest, but I just can't seem to get a commitment." There are at least four reasons why this happens. The first one I'm going to talk about here. The others I'll talk about in the following chapters.

Let me relate to you an actual experience I had. Several years back, I was approached by a man who had invented a rather unique sport craft. I'm not going to be any more specific because he may end up reading this book (I hope he does—he could use the help!). I went with a couple of associates of mine to meet him, and we all thought that what he had developed was a sure-fire winner. If this product could be brought to market, it would be a tremendous success. But the invention was not new. This gentleman had developed the product some years ago. He had built prototypes and even had them reviewed in some sports magazines. So, what had happened? Over the course of a few more meetings, it became increasingly apparent that this individual was the "mad scientist" and was no more fit to run a business than a chicken (yes, the kind that lays eggs). He was unfocused, contradictory, unprofessional, and bizarre. Now, to give him some credit, he may have been able to run the business, because in thinking more about it, I have known CEOs who fit all those descriptions. But in this case, he needed to raise money, and a lot of it, to get this product into production and to market it. Over many years, he had been unable to do so. I am convinced the reason he could not raise money was that he was his biggest impediment. So, thinking I was doing the professional thing, I took him to lunch, explained that I was certain money could be found for his deal, but that we might consider some other alternatives, such as licensing the product to a manufacturer already in business, forming a joint venture with someone, or alternatively bringing in a professional manager to move the business forward. You would have thought I had stolen his invention based on his reaction. Our meeting ended on a sour note, and I didn't see the gentlemen for about five years. I bumped into him at a financial conference. And guess what? He was still trying to raise money.

The point I am making here is that, with many businesses, the leader is an issue. Money guys are very hesitant to put money into a deal, if they think that the CEO of the company will not be able to run the company. They like to see a track record. That's why you often see people who sell off their successful company being able to start a new venture shortly thereafter, and it seems as if everyone on Wall Street is throwing money at them. It's the old story of betting on a winning horse. Now I know from experience that there are some excellent businesspeople out there. But there are also a lot of folks who got lucky, who were in the right place at the right time, or who otherwise found themselves at the head of a successful company whose success had nothing to do with them. Nevertheless, they get the credit for it, and Wall Street will give them the money. The fact is that many of these businesspeople fail in their next venture. That story usually finds its way to the small print on the back page of the business section.

Money guys are also very reluctant to put money into an enterprise that has had a setback if the management team remains the same. I was once helping a company raise capital that had taken a few missteps and lost some money. In this case, I thought the CEO was a good CEO and that the problems the company had were not directly related to his leadership. I found several interested funding sources, but each one was adamant about there being a change in management. The feeling is that a new broom sweeps clean, and the money guys are willing to give a new kid on the block a chance that they won't give to someone whom they perceive as having failed.

Both scenarios are a problem if you're the CEO of the company, and you have to question if the way the money guys perceive you is hampering the ability of your company to raise capital. And unfortunately, it is not something the money guys will tell you. They will end each meeting with a lot of "good stuff" and "nice presentation" and "we'll get back to you." But they won't come out and say, typically, you need a change in management before we put any money into the company. There are exceptions to that, of course, and I have heard of private equity funds that have agreed to fund deals based upon them orchestrating a change of management. But as often as not, if they perceive that the CEO is going to be a problem, they pass.

If you are the CEO of your company, and you are not willing to accept the fact that you may be the problem, then you might as well skip to the next chapter. For those CEOs who are a little more open, there are some solutions. First, do some real soul searching. How badly do you need to be the CEO anyway? Often it's a thankless job with a lot of hard work and risk. Maybe another role in the company would suit you better. If you're great with customers, maybe head of sales. If you're great with technology, maybe head of operations. If you're a mad scientist, maybe the head of product development. I know of a former CEO of a very large bio-medical company who, in the company's heyday, was living in a $15 million home in Beverly Hills. He was a scientist and doctor who pioneered certain medical tests.

The company got funded through a venture fund, and the company's stock went through the roof. Unfortunately, he wasn't too well suited for life in the executive suite. Some improprieties cost him his job and his fortune, and the Securities and Exchange Commission had him in jail for a period of time. If you can live without being CEO, then either find someone else to run the company, or if that is not practical due to finances or other issues, include in your business plan that once funded, you will search for a successor. You can even suggest to the money guys you meet that your strengths are not in the challenging position of CEO, and once the company has the capital and reaches a certain stage, you want them to replace you with someone else.

If you do that soul searching, and you still want to be CEO, but you wonder if you are the problem, you need to talk to someone who will give you a straight answer (this is something we'll talk more about in a later chapter). Find someone who will do a rational and brutally honest assessment of the way you appear to a money guy and tell you if you are the problem. You can also ask some of the folks who have declined to fund you if you personally had anything to do with their decision not to move forward. However, people are hesitant to say negative things, so if they say a lot of nice things, they might be holding back the truth. If you get negative feedback, take it to heart, but don't be fooled by a lot of praise—people hand out praise to be nice, even if they don't mean it. Haven't you ever said, "Dinner was great!" when in fact, the food was mediocre. Of course, we all have.

Assuming you still want to be CEO, and the person you choose to give you an honest answer suggests everything about you is just fine, consider changing your presentation style. In most presentations, I believe that one person should do most, if not all, the talking. Other members of the group can be along for support, or to answer specific questions in their area of expertise, but the CEO should hold center stage. However, I have seen, on several occasions, where a team approach got a much better response. It may have been the contrasting personality styles, it may have been that those people worked better as a team, or it may have been that the pressure was off when the CEO had a partner. If you typically do most of the talking in presentation meetings, try letting someone else on your team step into the limelight. It may result in significant differences in the way your presentation is perceived, and the interest level from prospective funding sources.

IT'S MY JOB

Another reason that you're getting a lot of interest but never raising the money is that you are talking to the wrong people. Now, this is where the CEO generally tells me that he or she has been to New York four times this year, each time had five great meetings, and in each of those meetings the people he/she met with showed considerable interest and said they would give the opportunity due consideration. I would still say you are meeting with the wrong people. Now the exasperated CEO wonders why these people would bother meeting with him/her, and be so interested in the deal, if they were the wrong people. It's simple. That's their job. Let me repeat that—it's their job.

There are two rules you need to know about funding sources. The first one is that funding sources; whether it's your local banker down the street, a hard moneylender, or an investment banker from Wall Street, all put their capital into deals that fit a certain profile. A traditional banker may want five years' operating history and three years of profits, a hard money lender may want accounts receivable and inventory that covers 70 percent of their advances, a private equity fund may want a projected 35 percent annualized return on their investment, and a venture capital fund may only invest in companies in a certain region of the country. The investment or lending formula of a capital source is typically corporate policy, and in some cases, may even be written into the funding source's charter or regulated by government legislation. They rarely deviate from this predetermined approach to putting their capital to work. Therefore, while it never hurts to talk to someone who is not going to fund your deal (we'll talk about this more a little later), you can waste a lot of time talking to people who are never going to fund your deal.

The second rule is that the money guys get paid to meet with people who are looking for money. Let me give you an example. A good friend of mine is the vice president of what I would call a traditional business bank. This bank specializes in what the industry calls mid-market clients. They know they'll never be the main bankers for General Motors, but on the other hand, they don't want to be banking the local dry cleaner—there's not enough money in it. They understand that businesses with revenues of between $10 million and maybe $200 million are companies that need more specialized service than you might get from a consumer bank, and businesses from which you can make a lot of profit. Now my friend spends most of his day visiting companies, taking the CEOs to lunch, going to presentations, networking, and the like. His goal? Meet as many target companies as he can and pitch his bank's services. Does he qualify every potential client before wasting his time meeting with them? Not on your life. "Why not?" you ask. For several reasons. First, even if he cannot lend the company any money, he knows that a lot of businesses get financing from other sources—non-bank financial institutions, equity investors, hard money lenders, and so on. So, even if he doesn't loan you the money, you will still need a banking relationship for traditional services like checking and deposit accounts, and maybe he can win you over to his bank. Second, you may not meet his bank's lending criteria today, but that may change. You may grow, your business may become more profitable, your revenues may increase, and he is hoping when that happens, you'll give him a call. Third, part of being on top of what's going on in an industry is talking with business owners—what companies are doing well, and what companies are not; what are the trends; where is the next crop of mid-market companies going to come from? Fourth, that's what he's paid to do. How do you think it goes over if my friend was to go to his boss, the president of the bank, and say, "Well George, didn't meet with any companies all week...could not find any worth meeting with." He'd be looking for a job faster than you can say Jack Flash.

Similarly, with investment bankers, fund managers, and analysts, these guys get big paychecks for meeting with companies. Yes, they also get paid by funding companies, but you can make a lot of money by funding only a handful of companies. So, what do you do with the rest of your time? You meet with companies. Maybe the fund manager invested in a regional retailer of prepaid cellular service a year ago. That company was doing $20 million a year and was in California. Your company is in the same business, but only doing $2 million a year, and in Idaho. Chances are you're going to get a meeting, even though this fund has a rule that it never invests in companies with revenues less than $10 million. Why is he going to meet with you? Maybe he can get the company he invested in previously to buy you, or maybe he wants some insider information on what's happening in the industry, or maybe he just wants to compare your performance with that of a company in which he previously invested. Regardless of the reason, you've got a 90 percent chance of getting a meeting with this guy, and about a 0 percent chance of getting your funding.

So, what is the answer? Simple...whenever you set up a meeting with a funding source, qualify the funding source first. That means asking how they approach deploying their capital, what kind of deals they have funded recently, and realistically what are your chances given their specific investment criteria. You may still want to meet with them. First, you never know— exceptions occur. And second, you can always use another opportunity to hone your presentation skills. But I would suggest you look realistically at the ways in which companies deploy capital and focus your energies on those companies most likely to fund your deal.

I want to re-emphasize this section. Why? Because I have explained this to countless CEOs who just don't get it. Let me put it very simply. Let's say you have a company that has great receivables, fast turning inventory, but due to your aggressive growth campaigns, you are unprofitable. Chances are you won't get financing from any major bank whose name you easily recognize, like Bank of America, Wells Fargo, US Bank, Chase Bank, and similar institutions. Well, let's rephrase that. You might get financing if you sign a personal guarantee and put up the $500,000 in equity in your house as security, but your business will not qualify for a loan. You need to look elsewhere.

No matter how many appeals to logic you make, no matter how great your deal looks on paper, no matter how eloquently you present your business proposition, you're not getting the money. All the money guys want to do is to take your deal, compare it to their box, and if you don't fit the box, they move on to the next deal. They never worry or even think about what the scenario might have looked like if they were just a little more flexible in their approach. Therefore, search out funding sources whose capital deployment formula fits with your business.

A SHEEP IN WOLF'S CLOTHING

Now let's move on to the third reason that you seem to be getting a lot of interest, but not raising the money. You may have a great business or business plan, be profitable, have great management, and superior strategy, but no matter how many presentations you give, you just can't seem to get the funding you need. This section probably applies more to companies looking for equity and equity/debt combinations than for companies looking for straight debt; where the focus is more on cash flow and value of the security, but even then, it can apply (I will give an example of that shortly).

The problem may be that your business is not in favor. Hang on a second. What do I mean by favor? Don't capital sources make their investment decision based on the hard, cold facts and an in-depth analysis of the business plan, the numbers, and the market? The simple answer is No!!! The investment community, in many cases, acts more like sheep than like wolves. Fund managers, analysts, investment bankers, venture capitalists, and all the other sordid characters that operate in the funding world follow the trends. These guys hang out in the same bars, they frequent the same country clubs, they are often members of the same alumni association, and they attend the same conferences. I remember back in the late nineties, anything to do with the Internet was a sure-fire winner. In 2004, any deal involving real estate was king. Now, it seems any-thing to do with energy and green technologies, artificial intel-ligence, remote work, or Blockchain is the way to go. This may sound simplistic, but it is not. Let me give you an example.

I was involved in the funding of a medical technology com-pany several years ago. The investment banker we were dealing with at the time introduced us to four Wall Street funds. We had meetings with two of them and talked with the other two by phone. You would think each one of these funds would be ana-lyzing our information independently, comparing it with their own portfolios and available capital, talking to their own fund-ing committees for a decision, and deciding based on the known facts. In fact, the first fund agreed to do the deal. When the other three funds found out that fund number one was in, they all jumped on board the ship like there was no tomorrow—so much for analytical, well thought out decision-making.

The reality on Wall Street is that the money follows the trends and the leaders. Those Wall Street wolves are actually sheep. If Big Dog Fund invests in totem poles, Little Dog Fund will do the same. If some funds are investing in fiber optics, chances are all the funds will be investing in fiber optics.

So, what does this mean to someone trying to raise money? If possible, hook your deal into the popular trends. It may be hard to do, but it may not be as difficult as you think. As I said to many companies back in the '90s, if you're a bathtub manufacturer looking for money, I suggest your business plan include a significant discussion of how you are going to sell your bathtubs over the Internet. Today, such terms as Blockchain, nanotechnology, social media, cannabis, and green technology are popular with investors. To make this point simple, find out where the money guys are putting their money, and see if there is any way to modify your story so that it resembles the deals they are doing—even if you have to stretch it a little to make the connection. It's well worth doing and could be the difference between the capital you need, and not getting the money.

Now you may be thinking that this type of situation only applies to companies looking for equity. However, that is not entirely true. I was involved with a company several years ago in the video production and distribution business. We had transferred our business to a regional business bank because this particular bank had made a great presentation on how they understood the film and video production business, how they had specialists on their team who were experts in the field, and how one of their goals was to be a major banker of film and video production companies. Three short years later, the bank asked us to find another lender to pay off the loans we had to this bank. Why? Was it because of our business? Our business had not changed at all. But apparently, the bank had changed. For whatever reason, film and video production were out of favor, and the bank was now chasing other businesses. We just didn't fit their mold any longer. Arbitrarily, for no good financial reason, a solid business account was being thrown out the door. Through a confidential conversation with someone on the inside, I later found out what had happened. The bank had brought in a new senior guy from another bank. This guy had no understanding of the film and video business, and when one of their customers in the business had a few hiccups, that was it. Their new focus turned to manufacturing and distribution companies.

A similar situation happened to me when helping a construction company trying to borrow working capital. This company had been in business for 70 years; the owners had accumulated a large real estate portfolio; the company was growing and was profitable. We had a banker, but we were shopping to see what the competition might offer. A large California business banker courted us and even gave us a soft proposal. We were on our way to changing banks. Then, suddenly, the banker called saying the orders had just come down from "on high" that the bank was no longer funding construction companies.

The lesson here is that you increase your chances of getting funding if the funding source is already lending or investing in your type of business. And if the funding source is not investing in your type of business, find out what they are investing in, and see if you can tweak your storyline just a little, to appeal to their sheep mentality.

WORTH EVERY PENNY

The fourth reason why you may not have gotten funding is that you are simply unrealistic in what you are willing to give up for the money that a money guy is willing to put in. This is one of the biggest deal killers of them all. It's not so significant in a lending scenario, as opposed to an equity investment, but even in a lending situation, unrealistic expectations of the price of capital can be the downfall of getting funded.

There are a few simple rules about the cost of money. Money is expensive, and the money guys control the price. The golden rule is, "He with the gold makes the rules." I have seen too many companies walk away from a funding source, thinking they would get a better deal somewhere else, only to find there was no other deal to be had; and by the time they agreed to do the original deal, their circumstances had changed, and the money guys were no longer interested (we'll talk more about this later).

Money guys understand that terms and conditions have some flexibility, but they need to be within a certain bandwidth. If the money guys think you will be reasonable in what you are willing to give up in terms of equity, security, control, repayment, interest rates, advance rates, and other factors, and if they like the deal, they'll make you a proposal. But if they think you are unrealistic or pig-headed, they won't even bother to put a deal on the table. They think it's just a waste of time, and they would rather move on to the next deal.

So, what exactly are we talking about? Let me give you a few examples. Sometime back, I was working with a small technology company. I made an introduction to a potential funding source that seemed interested. I had told the CEO that if the topic of valuation came up, to avoid the question, or to say he was flexible. This CEO was looking for $5 million. At some point in the conversation, the money guy asked, "So, Tom, if I write you a check for five million dollars, what do I get?"

Completely ignoring my advice, the CEO looked MG straight in the eye and said, "I'm thinking twenty percent of the company."

Do the math. If 20 percent is worth $5 million, then 100 percent is worth $25 million, and this company was not worth anywhere near $25 million. Now to put this in perspective, the company had no revenues, one employee, and a couple of prototype products. Even though the company did have a couple of interesting patents, those patents were of questionable value because until the products were brought to market, there was uncertainty as to how those products would be accepted. Even with very aggressive projections, it would take years for this company to achieve a $25 million valuation based on normal valuation models.

Right off the bat, this makes the CEO look like a fool, and that he has unrealistic expectations. The money guy rolled his eyes, the meeting ended, and all further attempts to get this guy interested were unsuccessful.

I know this topic is a tender one for most CEOs and business owners. After all, when the company was in its infancy, the top boys had to put in the time, energy, and ingenuity to get the company to where it is today, and that's worth something. Plus, executives often point to the outrageous valuations paid by huge corporations in Wall Street takeovers. Those are legitimate observations, but sometimes you are better not airing them. On occasion, you may be in a position where an investor or a lender overvalued your business, overestimates your earnings and growth potential, or overestimates your ability to pay back the debt. Lucky you when it happens, and if it happens, take full advantage of it. But don't expect it to happen, and most of all, don't talk to the money guys about expectations that the money guys will perceive as unrealistic, because it will reflect poorly on you, and then your chance of getting a deal done will decrease.

The next example is one of my favorites because it involves the former CEO of a division of a Fortune 100 company. It's one of my favorite examples because a lot of executives and owners of bigger companies think the advice in my book is for beginners—small companies, young entrepreneurs, start-ups, and the like—because after all, seasoned executives in big companies have been through the ropes, have all the right credentials, and know how the world works...right? Wrong!! Some of them do, but more than enough are bunglers and incompetents. All you have to do is read the *Wall Street Journal* for a few days to see that—companies overpay for an acquisition, only to sell it off for pennies on the dollar a year or two later because they couldn't run it; disastrous expansions into new markets; introductions of new products with great fanfare that never sell; settlements in huge lawsuits for ignoring ethical and moral operating standards; and the list goes on and on. Take a company that's worth $1 billion, and take a company that's worth $10 million, and I can assure you that every day of the week that billion-dollar company is making dumb, avoidable mistakes that would put the $10 million company out of business in a heartbeat.

Back to our example...this former CEO of the division of a Fortune 100 company had started a business in which he had the expertise, for which there was a ready market, for which there were some unique but extremely positive competitive advantages, and which would make any investor a lot of money. But the company was a startup, and even though the CEO had put some of his and his friend's capital into the business, they needed a very large investment. We found a private equity fund that was interested, also, had the money to do the deal, and had significant expertise in the business sector. Everything looked great. However, in the first phone meeting with the fund's analyst, the topic of control had come up. The CEO was adamant that he was not giving up control under any circumstances. Now, sometimes, to get the capital you need, particularly if you are a startup, you may have to give up control. But even if you don't give up control, you need to approach the money guys with an aura of flexibility and compromise. I think this CEO simply had "Fortune-100-itis." He was so used to the big stick he carried as the CEO of a division of a Fortune 100 company that he didn't realize how to behave in a different context and situation.

We were able to schedule an "in-person" meeting with Mr. Big at the fund. That was quite an achievement, and certainly a strong indication that there was significant interest. I had recommended to the CEO that if the issue of control came up, he should waffle a little—say he was flexible, say he was open to any reasonable deal structure, say a lot depended upon the amount of capital forthcoming, etcetera. Unfortunately, at that meeting, when the topic of control came up, the CEO went in the opposite direction, and in as belligerent a manner as I have experienced, said in no uncertain terms that he would not even give a deal that didn't leave him in control a minute's worth of his attention. Mr. Big, feathers ruffled, spent the next fifteen minutes attacking the CEO's business plan and strategy, and then abruptly ended the meeting. Since that time, the fund has made numerous other investments in that business sector, and the CEO never did raise the capital. The market conditions turned, and his business became far less lucrative. The sad part is that it may have been possible to structure a deal that accomplished both parties' objectives, because at the end of the day, what the CEO wanted was not to have someone telling him how to run his business, and what Mr. Big wanted was to ensure there was a mechanism in place to protect the downside if the business went south.

My third example involves debt. I was working with a company that needed to raise some money. The company had been in business for a few years but had had some ups and downs. To me, I thought the company should take on an equity investor, as it was uncertain if the company would generate enough cash flow to service debt. The owner was adamant that he didn't want to give up any equity. I found a lender that specialized in higher-risk situations, who was willing to advance the funds. However, the assets of the company really were not great security, and the lender wanted a personal guarantee from the owner. The owner, who over the years had taken millions of dollars out of business, had a substantial real estate portfolio and net worth. However, he adamantly refused to sign a personal guarantee. As a result, the lender passed, and the company did not get any financing. Six months later, the owner ended up having to sell the company to a competitor at fire-sale prices.

The moral of these stories is simple. Understand the way the money guy you are talking to invests, stay flexible and open-minded, and be realistic. If you think your business is worth $20 million, have some analysis or calculation to support that number. If you want to keep control, look at similar deals that have been done with other companies to see if their founders were able to keep control. If you don't want to sign personal guarantees, find what kind of financial strength a bank needs from a borrower to waive personal guarantees.

Business brokers, CPAs, investment bankers, and many

others can give you some basic guidelines as to what a business in your industry is worth and what kind of deals typically get done—ten times net profit, five times cash flow, two times revenue, $50 for each customer, 70 percent loan to value. Knowing and understanding these guidelines is a great help in getting a deal done, and in getting the best deal, you can without coming across as an arrogant or inflexible businessperson.

WHAT'S THE DEAL?

At some point, after you've supplied a funding source with your initial package of information (business plan, two-pager, product literature, financial projections, and historical financials), the funding source is going to decide it wants to move further, or pass on the deal. If the funding source wants to move further, then this is the time when you should get a term sheet or commitment letter explaining how the deal is going to be structured. The normal flow of a money transaction typically follows a very similar pattern. First, the opportunity, whether debt or equity, is presented in written form and in a face-to-face presentation. Second, a term letter or commitment letter is signed. In some instances, a money guy may ask for some additional information, or another meeting, before actually putting together the term sheet, but the term sheet should be forthcoming before the due diligence process is started (see the chapter on due diligence). If the money guys don't give you a term sheet, but continually ask for more information, be suspicious—we'll talk more about this later. Once the term sheet is signed, the due diligence process begins. As the due diligence process comes to completion, documents are drawn up; and when the fine print in the documents has been agreed upon, funding occurs.

The term sheet outlines the general structure of the deal. If it were a loan, it would include interest rate, principal amount, security, repayment terms, and perhaps some key covenants the company must comply with to get the money. If it is equity, it could include the price per share, the number of shares, restrictions on the issuance of additional shares, re-pricing issues, and other relevant provisions (see sample term sheets at the end of this chapter).

Term sheets or commitment letters are not binding agree-ments in terms of the funding. They are always subject to due diligence and to the preparation of final documents. However, there may be certain clauses in a term sheet that are binding, and that can cost you time, money, and even opportunity.

In some cases, funding sources may ask for an up-front due diligence fee so they can pay for their cost of doing the due dili-gence. This type of fee is especially annoying when the funding source has the opportunity for any reason, or no reason, not to fund, but keeps the due diligence fee. Recognize you may have to pay such fees, but always try to negotiate them, so they are as low as possible, or refundable if the funding source walks away from the deal.

Another common clause in a term sheet is a no-shop clause, in which you give the funding source the opportunity to do its due diligence, during which time you agree not to talk to any other funding sources. Be careful about this clause. I would rather pay a breakup fee (a fee that pays the funding source enough to cover its trouble) if I decide to use another funding source, than enter into an agreement to stop talking to other funding sources. At best, limit such a clause to a few weeks, because the fact is that a large portion of deals falls through in the due diligence process, and due diligence can take months of time, particularly for larger, more established companies.

Another common clause is a confidentiality or non-dis-closure clause. This clause keeps you from divulging the terms of the term sheet or commitment letter to other funding sources—in other words, shopping the funding source's offer to other funding sources while the original funding source does its due diligence. If you are faced with this clause in a term sheet, limit it to a certain time frame, such as thirty days, to make sure the funding source does its due diligence quickly.

If you are already talking to other funding sources and you think any of them are close to a deal, before signing the term sheet, let the other funding sources know you have a term sheet, and what it would take to get you to do a deal with them. Now, this is a different situation than what we discussed before in terms of not being too specific about what type of a deal you're looking for. Take the term sheet you have, improve the terms by 5 to 15 percent in your favor, and then mention to these other funding sources that you'd be happy to do a deal if the deal looked like the improved deal that you've come up with. To give them some time to think about it, this would be a great time to head off to the cottage in the woods for a couple of days of fishing, so you can't be pushed into signing the original term sheet before the competitors have a chance to come in with something better.

The term sheet should contain a mutual confidentiality agreement under which the funding source agrees to keep anything you provide confidential, including the fact that it has issued you a term sheet. In some instances, it can be problematic if competitors or other funding sources you currently deal with find out that you are talking to other folks.

There are three things to be very cautious of at the term sheet stage of funding. The first one is the funding source that can never get to a term sheet. If the money guys don't give you a term sheet, but continually ask for more information, be suspicious. I've seen this go on for months. Every couple of days, the money guys want more info, want to talk to more people, want to do more research, and for some reason, the term sheet never comes. It may be they never plan to give you a term sheet anyway. They will be three-quarters of the way through the due diligence, with still no term sheet, when finally they'll say they can't help you. If you press them why, you will often be told that it is because of something they have discovered in the process, but in further analysis, you will discover that the one thing they have a problem with, is something they should have known, or could have asked right up front. They have simply used the process to find out more information about your business. It is doubtful that they will steal any of your customers or great ideas, but if they are a funding source that funds a number of companies in your same business, they may use this chance to get more information on the industry, the way it works, standards of performance in the industry, and other useful information. The fact that they got this information, however, is not a big deal. <u>The big deal is that they have wasted weeks, maybe months of your time, when you could have been dancing with another funding source.</u>

The second thing to be cautious of is what I call the "deal killers." These include those things that are so critical to the way a funding source does business, that if they discovered certain things, they would not do the deal. You need to ask this question and preferably get it in writing. I was involved in funding one time for a healthcare company. The funding source was provided with a package of information upfront—the information that we have talked about in this book. The funding source liked the deal and put forth a term sheet that required an up-front $25,000 due diligence fee. The company paid the fee, and the funding source began two months of due diligence. At the end of the two months, the whole deal went to the final approval stage, and was turned down. The reason? One of the principals of the company had been sued in a civil action, and had settled the lawsuit out of court—you know, the kind of settlement where nobody admits anything, but it's cheaper to settle the suit than to pay the attorneys. OK, if that is their reason, that's their reason. Then it dawned on me. The details of this entire suit had been well documented in the original package sent to the funding source, prior to them even presenting a commitment letter. I complained vehemently to the head fund manager at this very large lending organization to no avail. The company could not get its money back. I wonder how much of that funding source's revenue is due diligence fees on deals they never fund?

The third thing to watch out for is the advisor, in particular attorneys, who think that the term sheet is their opportunity to negotiate all the terms and conditions of the final deal. The term sheet, by its very nature, does not include every detail of the deal. It is a summary at the highest level. The term sheet assumes that if you can agree on the big picture, then you will be able to work out the niggles during the due diligence and documentation stage. For whatever reason, some people (in particular, some attorneys) just don't get that. I was working with one company that received a term sheet from a non-bank lender. The deal looked pretty good from my perspective. However, the CEO of the company was not going one-step further without having his attorney scrutinize the term sheet. It took two weeks to come up with the final term sheet. It was the longest-term sheet I had ever seen, and it included a list of terms and details normally only seen in the final documents. I recall this attorney crowing about what a great job he had done. The lender signed off on the term sheet and began the due diligence. Two days into the due diligence, they passed on the deal, and for very legitimate reasons. The $10,000 the company had spent with the attorney on the term sheet went right down the drain. The lesson here is that you must make sure you rein in your attorneys, so they aren't racking up fees unnecessarily. If your attorney spends any more than an hour on the term sheet—he's probably taking you for a ride.

Once you have a signed term sheet, the due diligence process begins, and that's covered in the next chapter.

The following are samples of a few real terms sheets from deals that I have worked on. Obviously, the terms of the deal, and even the information written in the term sheet, will vary depending upon the circumstances of each specific deal and who is involved in the transaction, but by reviewing these sample term sheets, you'll begin to get an idea of what you should be expecting from funding sources when they get to the term sheet stage. You will note that some are written more simply, and some are much more complex. The amount of detail included in a term sheet is often determined by the pattern or style of the funding source. There is no right answer as to how much detail should be included in the term sheet. Rather you should make sure that the general concepts outlined in the term sheet are understandable, and that you can live with them. There is plenty of time to negotiate the small print after the due diligence process is completed, and when you are working on the final definitive documents.

SAMPLE TERM SHEET #1

This term sheet was presented to my client and me by an investment-banking firm that had agreed to raise my client $5 million to start an opportunistic investment fund. These were the terms under which the investment-banking firm was willing to raise this capital.

NO-NAME CAPITAL, INC.

$5,000,000 of Convertible Secured Notes

The Issuer: No-Name Capital, Inc. ("No-Name") is in the business of identifying and deploying capital for high yield, asset secured, and opportunistic investments. Investment targets include bankrupt and foreclosed assets, accounts receivable factoring, purchase order financing, bridge loans to public or soon to be, public companies, "hard money" real estate loans, payday loans, and other one-off funding opportunities. No Name intends to raise an initial $5,000,000 for the purpose of making investments in applicable opportunities.

Public Status: No-Name is not yet trading. No-Name expects to be fully reporting and trading by December 31, 2007.

Securities Offered: Up to $5,000,000 aggregate face amount 10% Convertible Secured Notes (the "Notes") plus warrants to purchase an aggregate $2,500,000 of the Company's common stock (the "Warrants"); collectively referred to as the "Securities."

Minimum Investment: $25,000 per purchaser

Use of Proceeds: 90% of the proceeds raised from this offering must be held in cash, near cash equivalents, or invested in target investment opportunities. 10% may be used for expenses associated with this offering, including commissions, and general overhead of the Company.

Principal: The entire unpaid principal amount of each Note will be due and payable on the thirty-six (36) month anniversary of the Closing Date.

Interest Rate: Interest will accrue on each Note from Closing Date at the rate of ten percent (10%) per annum. Accrued interest will be paid quarterly in cash or in Common Stock, at the Company's option.

Optional Conversion: Each Note will be convertible into Common Stock at the option of the holder at any time after the first six months following the closing, in whole or in part, at a 50% discount to market, such that for each $1.00 in face value of the Note, the holder will be entitled to purchase $2.00 of common stock based on the trading price of the stock at the time of the election.

Mandatory
Conversion: The Company will have the ability to cause the Investors to convert their Notes into Common Stock if (i) twelve months have elapsed since the Closing date AND (ii) if the average daily volume for Common Stock during the twenty (20) consecutive day period preceding the Mandatory Conversion exceeds 50,000 shares.

Warrant Coverage: For each $1.00 in the face value of the Note, the holder will be entitled to purchase an equivalent amount of stock at a thirty percent (30%) to the market at the time of exercise. Warrants Share have net exercise provision and term of 3 years.

Investor Suitability: The Units shall only be sold to Accredited Investors and Institutional Investors as defined by Rule 501 of Regulation D under the Securities Act of 1933, as amended.

Management: President and Chief Financial Officer
                       Executive Vice President
                       Vice President - Operations
Security: The holders of the Convertible Secured Notes will hold a Security Interest in all the assets of the Company senior to all other debt instruments except a conventional bank line of credit limited to $500,000.

Memorandum and
Sub. Agreement: Each prospective investor will be provided with an Agreement for the Purchase and Suitability Form. To participate in the Convertible Secured Notes, each investor must complete and execute the Securities Purchase Agreement and tender payment as set forth therein. The Securities Purchase

Agreement shall not be binding until acceptance and execution thereof by the Manager. The Manager reserves the right to reject any Securities Purchase Agreement for any reason, at its sole discretion.

**Placement Fees
And Expenses:** Management estimates fees, commissions, and/or finder's fees associated with this offering may be as much as 10% of monies invested, but the actual percentage may be more or less.

SAMPLE TERM SHEET #2

This term sheet was received by my client, who was looking for a line of credit to finance its increasing accounts receivable.

REVOLVING CREDIT LINE

Amount:	$2,000,000
Type:	Revolving Fixed Convertible Note
Coupon:	WSJ Prime plus 3%
Term:	3 years

Formula: $2,000,000 in availability will be based on Accounts Receivable at an advance rate of up to 90% of eligible receivables.

Over-advance: Upon closing of a transaction with XXXXX, a $300,000 one-time over-advance will be made available.

Equity Component: The structure allows for a portion of the outstanding balance to be converted into equity, thus creating additional availability under the facility and simultaneously increasing the funding amounts available to the Company.

Conversion: The Fixed Conversion Price to convert the debt to equity will be $1.10 per share. The lender may convert any portion of the principal outstanding to equity if the market price is 110% of the Fixed Conversion Price, subject to a maximum conversion of $100,000 in any 30-day period.

Registration: The Company will file a registration statement for the Company's common stock underlying the financing and all underlying warrants with the SEC within 150 days of funding.

Termination: An early termination fee of 4% applies if the facility is terminated in its entirety before maturity.

Collateral: First lien on accounts receivable.

Fees: A closing fee of 4%, an annual renewal fee of 1%.

Warrants: Five-year warrants as follows:
150,000 at 110% of Fixed Conversion Price
100,000 at 120% of Fixed Conversion Price
75,000 at 130% of Fixed Conversion Price.

SAMPLE TERM SHEET #3

This sample term sheet was provided to me by an investment-banking firm as the standard template that the company used for making investments in various companies.

CONFIDENTIAL MEMORANDUM TERM SHEET

[COMPANY NAME]
Convertible Debentures and Warrants

This confidential memorandum summarizes the principal terms of the proposed investment in [COMPANY NAME] (the "Company"). This memorandum is for discussion purposes only. The completion of the transactions contemplated by this memorandum will be subject to, among other things, satisfactory completion of financial and legal due diligence by the Purchaser, as well as the completion of final documents acceptable to the Purchaser and the Company.

Amount: $XXXXXX, to be funded upon Initial Closing, and subject to customary conditions.

Purchaser: [INVESTOR]

Securities: Convertible Debentures, convertible into shares of common stock ("Common Stock") of the Company, issued pursuant to the private placement exemption under U.S. securities laws.

Warrants: On the Initial Closing Date, the Purchaser shall receive warrants to purchase XXXXXX shares of Common Stock with an exercise price per share equal to the closing bid price on the trading day immediately preceding the Initial Closing Date, with provisions for cashless exercise at the Purchaser's option and customary anti-dilution protections. The warrants will expire on the fifth anniversary of the Initial Closing Date.

Closing Date: The Company and the Purchaser shall use their reasonable best efforts to consummate the Initial Closing on or before XXXX XX, 2020.

Maturity: The Convertible Debentures shall mature on the second anniversary of the Initial Closing Date at a price equal to 125% of par plus accrued interest plus liquidated damages, if any.

Interest: 8% per annum, compounding semi-annually, payable in cash or freely tradable shares of Common Stock at the option of the Company.

Conversion Terms: The Convertible Debentures will be convertible, in whole or in part, into shares of Common Stock at any time at the option of the Purchaser.

Conversion Price: The Convertible Debentures will be convertible into Common Stock at a price equal to the lesser of: (a) 75% of the average of the closing bid prices of the Common Stock on the three trading days immediately preceding the Initial Closing Date and (b) 75% of the average of the three lowest closing bid prices of the Common Stock during the five trading days immediately preceding the Conversion Date.

Security: At the Initial Closing, XXXXXX unrestricted shares of Common Stock shall be placed in escrow with the Purchaser's representative. The obligations of the Company set forth below under "Registration Rights" will be secured by a pledge of such shares, which shall have been held for at least two years by one or more existing shareholders of the Company who have not been affiliates of the Company within the prior 90 days... Such pledgers shall waive all rights of subrogation against the Company in respect of the pledge, and such shares shall be Rule 144(k) eligible. If a registration statement covering the shares issuable upon conversion of the Convertible Debentures and exercise of the warrants has not been declared effective within 90 days following the Initial Closing Date, the Purchaser shall have the right to acquire the pledged shares in partial satisfaction of the Company's obligations under the Convertible Debentures. The pledged shares shall be governed by an Escrow Agreement.

**Registration
Rights:** The Common Stock underlying the securities (200% of the shares underlying the Convertible Debentures and 100% of the shares underlying the warrants) will be registered for resale as soon as possible after the Initial Closing Date. The Purchaser and the Company will enter into a Registration Rights Agreement providing, among other things, that the registration statement will be filed within 15 days of the Initial Closing Date. The Company will use its best efforts to cause the registration statement to become effective within 90 days following the Initial Closing Date. If the registration statement has not

been filed within 15 days following the Initial Closing Date or the registration statement has not been declared effective within 90 days from the Initial Closing Date, then the Company will be liable for liquidated damages enforceable by the Purchaser. The liquidated damages will be in the amount of 2% of the principal amount of the outstanding Convertible Debentures and the aggregate exercise price of the warrants for the first 30 days and 3% for every 30-day period thereafter until the registration statement has been filed or declared effective (as applicable). The liquidated damages will be payable in cash upon demand.

**Conditions
to Initial Closing:**

1. The Company shall be listed on OTCBB, NASDAQ, NYSE, or AMEX.
2. All executed documents and securities shall be received by the Purchaser.
3. The pledged shares shall be received by the Escrow Agent.

Fees: The Company shall pay the Placement Agent a cash fee equal to 10% of the principal amount of the Convertible Debentures, and shall issue to the Placement Agent Warrants to purchase XXXXXX worth of Common Stock at a price per share equal to the closing bid price on the day preceding the Initial Closing Date. These warrants shall have the same form as the Purchaser's warrants.

Legal Fees: At the Initial Closing, the Company shall pay the Purchaser's legal fees and expenses, not to exceed $20,000. In addition, if requested by the Company, the Company shall pay the legal fees and expenses of Purchaser's counsel for preparing the first draft of the registration statement, not to exceed $20,000.

Confidentiality: The Company agrees to treat this memo-randum confidentially and will not distrib-ute it or disclose its contents outside the Company.

BE DILIGENT FOR
THE DILIGENCE

Chances are, if you are looking for funding of any sort, you will be faced with the due diligence phase of the process. In the due diligence phase, you will provide the funding source all the additional documentation needed for the money guys to be happy with the deal. Whether it is debt or equity, they will want to look at financial statements, contracts, patents, inventory lists, accounts receivable lists, insurance policies, employment agreements, leases, distribution agreements, and more. They may want to talk with customers, suppliers, and employees. They may want to bring in industry experts to validate technologies or products. They will most likely run background and credit checks on key executives and owners. I am not going to elaborate on due diligence because I am assuming that most people reading this book will have some concept of due diligence and the due diligence process. What I am going to talk about is the timing of due diligence, and preparedness for due diligence, something that even large companies often don't handle well.

When a funding source likes your deal and is ready to put money on the table, it will typically prepare a term sheet or commitment letter, as mentioned in the previous chapter. Once that term sheet is signed, the funding source will typically supply a due diligence checklist (see sample due diligence checklist at the end of this chapter). In some cases, the Money Guys may ask for items that might typically be considered part of the due diligence information prior to providing a term sheet. Whether it is information you need to supply before you get a term sheet, or information you provide after signing the term sheet, for purposes of this chapter, we are going to consider all the information as part of the due diligence information. Here are the rules for due diligence information.

<u>Be prepared.</u> You should not wait until the lender or equity investor asks you for information to begin collecting and organizing it. In today's technology age, you should be prepared to deliver due diligence information in both electronic, and hard copy format. If you have not done so already, collect all your due diligence material (see a sample due diligence checklist at the end of this chapter) and scan every document into a computer file. Save all these files into one folder, and make sure that each one is properly labeled and that you have an index of files. This way, if a money guy wants one document, you can email it to him. If he wants the entire due diligence file, you can copy it to a memory stick or give access through the cloud. Today most companies use some form of cloud storage such as Google Docs, Microsoft OneDrive, or one of the other cloud-based storage services. In transactions where documents are stored on a cloud service the documents are often referred to as being in the "vault."

Remember, however, that not everyone likes electronic documents. So, you still need to have a complete due diligence file in hard copy format. And like your electronic file, it should be indexed. Make one master copy, and then as you need it, you can make copies of the master copy to send to the money guys. I would recommend maintaining your due diligence material on an ongoing basis, as much of this information could be needed for other activities (such as audits), and it's nice to have all of this information at your fingertips.

Now I can hear the CEOs of larger companies reading this section of the book and chortling away, thinking about how this applies to start-up companies and the like. Wrong!! In some larger companies, putting together due diligence information is a tremendous chore. The CEO thinks all documents are readily at hand and usually assigns the project to his secretary or administrative assistant. She then spends two weeks pulling her hair out because the employment agreements are in the bottom locked filing cabinet in the payroll office, the distribution agreements are in the sales manager's briefcase, the historical financial statements are in the CFO's left-hand desk drawer, and the insurance policy is in the big pile of stuff on the CEO's credenza because in his spare time he was going to review it. Further, the bigger the company, the more documents that typically form the due diligence information.

<u>Respond to due diligence requests on a timely basis.</u> This rule applies both to the main body of due diligence discussed above, as well as the special requests for information that may not be included in the due diligence checklist. Again, this is something bigger company CEOs will laugh at. They typically think it is the start-ups that can't do things on a timely basis. But often in the early-stage company, the CEO is intimately involved, and the success of the company is so dependent upon the capital, that the CEO is eager to jump on any request and get personally involved. In larger companies, information may have to come from different departments and different divisions, and the people responsible for providing that information may have very stressful and demanding jobs. Even larger companies that can quickly produce the main body of due diligence, often are very slow to deliver additional information, particularly if it requires more analytical work on the part of management.

So why is it important to respond quickly and to have well prepared due diligence material on hand? Because the money guys will judge you based on your ability to produce complete, accurate, and timely due diligence materials. Further, most money guys are working on several deals. If a deal slows down or stagnates because simple information is not forthcoming, then the money guys' interest begins to fade, and they turn their attention to other opportunities.

I was assisting one company in finding some funding sources. The company's sales were small, but the CEO and other executives constantly talked about the "pipeline"— business that was supposedly coming in. However, when the money guys asked to see an analysis of what was in this pipeline, no analysis was ever forthcoming. I soon lost confidence in management, and backed out of my role as an advisor, because I was no longer comfortable in introducing these clearly incapable executives to funding sources with which I had a relationship.

Another time I was working on a very large deal. I had introduced a good-sized financial services company to a private equity fund. After preliminary meetings, the fund asked for some additional information. I hounded the company for weeks for that information, and a month and a half later, when it was finally provided, the fund had lost interest in the deal and was working on a deal with one of this company's competitors.

So, the deal about due diligence is to have it ready and deliver it quickly. And if you get additional one-off requests, make answering those requests a top priority for you and your management team.

SAMPLE DUE DILIGENCE CHECKLIST

A. *Organization and Good Standing*

- ✓ The Company's Articles of Incorporation, and all amendments
- ✓ The Company's Bylaws, and all amendments
- ✓ The Company's minute book, including all minutes and resolutions of shareholders and directors, executive committees, and other governing groups
- ✓ The Company's organizational chart
- ✓ The Company's list of shareholders and number of shares held by each
- ✓ Copies of agreements relating to options, voting trusts, warrants, puts, calls, subscriptions, and convertible securities
- ✓ A Certificate of Good Standing from the Secretary of State of the state where the Company is incorporated
- ✓ Copies of the active status report in the state of incorporation for the last three years
- ✓ A list of all states where the Company is authorized to do business and annual reports for the last three years
- ✓ A list of all states, provinces, or countries where the Company owns or leases property, maintains employees or conducts business
- ✓ A list of all the Company's assumed names and copies of registrations

B. *Financial Information*

- ✓ Audited financial statements for three years, together with Auditor's Reports
- ✓ The most recent unaudited statements, with comparable statements to the prior year

- ✓ Auditor's letters and replies for the past five years
- ✓ The Company's credit report, if available
- ✓ Any projections, capital budgets, and strategic plans
- ✓ Analyst reports, if available
- ✓ A schedule of all indebtedness and contingent liabilities
- ✓ A schedule of inventory
- ✓ A schedule of accounts receivable
- ✓ A schedule of accounts payable
- ✓ A description of depreciation and amortization methods and changes in accounting methods over the past five years
- ✓ Any analysis of fixed and variable expenses
- ✓ An analysis of gross margins
- ✓ The Company's general ledger
- ✓ A description of the Company's internal control procedures

D. *Physical Assets*
- ✓ A schedule of fixed assets and their locations
- ✓ All U.C.C. filings
- ✓ All leases of equipment
- ✓ A schedule of sales and purchases of major capital equipment during the last three years

E. *Real Estate*
- ✓ A schedule of the Company's business locations
- ✓ Copies of all real estate leases, deeds, mortgages, title policies, surveys, zoning approvals, variances, or use permits

F. *Intellectual Property*
- ✓ A schedule of domestic and foreign patents and patent

applications

- ✓ A schedule of trademark and trade names
- ✓ A schedule of copyrights
- ✓ A description of important technical know-how
- ✓ A description of methods used to protect trade secrets and know-how
- ✓ Any "work for hire" agreements
- ✓ A schedule and copies of all consulting agreements, agreements regarding inventions, licenses, or assignments of intellectual property to or from the Company
- ✓ Any patent clearance documents
- ✓ A schedule and summary of any claims or threatened claims by or against the Company regarding intellectual property

G. *Employees and Employee Benefits*

- ✓ A list of employees including positions, current salaries, salaries, and bonuses paid during the last three years, and years of service
- ✓ All employment, consulting, nondisclosure, no solicitation, or noncompetition agreements between the Company and any of its employees
- ✓ Resumes of key employees
- ✓ The Company's personnel handbook and a schedule of all employee benefits and holiday, vacation, and sick leave policies
- ✓ Summary plan descriptions of qualified and non-qualified retirement plans
- ✓ Copies of collective bargaining agreements if any
- ✓ A description of all employee problems within the last three years, including alleged wrongful termination, harassment, and discrimination

✓ A description of any labor disputes, requests for arbitration, or grievance procedures currently pending or settled within the last three years

✓ A list and description of benefits of all employee health and welfare insurance policies or self-funded arrangements

✓ A description of worker's compensation claim history

✓ A description of unemployment insurance claims history

✓ Copies of all stock option and stock purchase plans and a schedule of grants

H. *Licenses and Permits*

✓ Copies of any governmental licenses, permits, or consents

✓ Any correspondence or documents relating to any proceedings of any regulatory agency

I. *Environmental Issues*

✓ Environmental audits, if any, for each property leased by the Company

✓ A listing of hazardous substances used in the Company's operations

✓ A description of the Company's disposal methods

✓ A list of environmental permits and licenses

✓ Copies of all correspondence, notices, and files related to EPA, state, or local regulatory agencies

✓ A list identifying and describing any environmental litigation or investigations

✓ A list identifying and describing any known Superfund exposure

✓ A list identifying and describing any contingent environmental liabilities or continuing indemnification obligations

J. *Taxes*

✓ Federal, state, local, and foreign income tax returns for the last three years

✓ States sales tax returns for the last three years

✓ Any audit and revenue agency reports

✓ Any tax settlement documents for the last three years

✓ Employment tax filings for three years

✓ Excise tax filings for three years

✓ Any tax liens

K. *Material Contracts*

✓ A schedule of all subsidiary, partnership, or joint venture relationships and obligations, with copies of all related agreements

✓ Copies of all contracts between the Company and any officers, directors, 5-percent shareholders, or affiliates

✓ All loan agreements, bank financing arrangements, line of credit, or promissory notes to which the Company is a party

✓ All security agreements, mortgages, indentures, collateral pledges, and similar agreements, including guaranties to which the Company is a party, and any installment sale agreements

✓ Any distribution agreements, sales representative agreements, marketing agreements, and supply agreements

✓ Any letters of intent, contracts, and closing transcripts from any mergers, acquisitions, or divestitures within the last five years

✓ Any options and stock purchase agreements involving interests in other companies

✓ The Company's standard quote, purchase order, invoice, and warranty forms

✓ All nondisclosure or noncompetition agreements to which the Company is a party

✓ All other material contracts

L. *Product or Service Lines*

✓ A list of all existing products or services and products or services under development

✓ Copies of all correspondence and reports related to any regulatory approvals or disapprovals of any Company's products or services

✓ A summary of all complaints or warranty claims

✓ A summary of results of all tests, evaluations, studies, surveys, and other data regarding existing products or services and products or services under development

M. *Customer Information*

✓ A schedule of the Company's twelve largest customers in terms of sales thereto and a description of sales thereto over a period of two years

✓ Any supply or service agreements

✓ A description or copy of the Company's purchasing policies

✓ A description or copy of the Company's credit policy

✓ A schedule of unfilled orders

✓ A list and explanation for any major customers lost over the last two years

✓ All surveys and market research reports relevant to the Company or its products or services

✓ The Company's current advertising programs, marketing plans, and budgets, and printed marketing materials

✓ A description of the Company's major competitors

N. *Litigation*
- ✓ A schedule of all pending litigation
- ✓ A description of any threatened litigation
- ✓ Copies of insurance policies possibly providing coverage as to pending or threatened litigation
- ✓ Documents relating to any injunctions, consent decrees, or settlements to which the Company is a party
- ✓ A list of unsatisfied judgments

O. *Insurance Coverage*
- ✓ A schedule and copies of the Company's general liability, personal and real property, product liability, errors and omissions, key-man, directors and officers, worker's compensation, and other insurance
- ✓ A schedule of the Company's insurance claims history for the past three years

P. *Professionals*
- ✓ A schedule of all law firms, accounting firms, consulting firms, and similar professionals engaged by the Company during the past five years

Q. *Articles and Publicity*
- ✓ Copies of all articles and press releases relating to the Company within the past three years

WHO'S IN THE MIDDLE?

An important decision in raising capital is whether to use an intermediary. And if you use one, how do you pick one, and exactly what services do you need? First, however, let's clarify some terms, because in the money-raising field, just who is who can be very confusing.

I refer to an intermediary as a person or company who assists in some way in raising the capital you need, or in getting you your loan—someone who is *not* putting the money in themselves. Now, you may ask, "Mike, why do you call them an intermediary? I thought they were investment bankers." Well, they may be investment bankers; but that term has been thrown around so much that it has almost become meaningless. Someone from Morgan Stanley working on a billion-dollar raise for General Motors calls himself an investment banker, yet I have gotten cards from individuals that say "investment banker" when these guys are one-man-shows working out of their living rooms. Now don't get me wrong, those one-man-shows can be very effective in helping find money, but I just want to clarify the services you might need in other terms that more clearly indicate whom you are dealing with and what you are getting— and more about the different kinds of intermediaries.

Many investment-banking firms are registered broker-dealers. This means they are registered with, are licensed by, and are monitored by the Financial Industry Regulatory Authority ("FINRA"). However, it is not necessarily the case that a FINRA registered broker-dealer is an investment banker, or that an investment banker is a FINRA registered broker-dealer ("BD"). A BD is licensed to trade securities and sell stocks, bonds, mutual funds, and other security instruments. They are also licensed to perform money-raising activities. However, many BDs choose not to get involved in money raising, but rather strictly stick to trading securities. On the other hand, there are many BDs that only engage in money raising, and don't trade securities. Being a BD is no indication of expertise in any specific financial areas because BDs can specialize in the type of securities trading and investment banking they do. Finally, being a BD does not reflect size. Morgan Stanley, with thousands of employees, is a BD. And I know a one-man-show who lives on a boat who is also a BD.

I break the intermediary's role down into two specific tasks. The first one is an advisory task for the company. Most companies that are raising funds need someone to review the business plan, financial projections, two-pager, presentation, and other information, and guide the company to put together these materials such that they tell a better story or are more cohesive or more realistic. He/she may coach the CEO on how to present and on what to say, and on what not to say, and how to say it. The advisor may also advise the company on potential deal structures, types of fundings available, what funding sources might be suitable candidates for the capital raise (Is this a loan from the local Bank of America, or do we need venture capital from one of those Silicon Valley venture funds?), and other valuable deal-related information. A good advisor might also be able to assist the company in negotiations with a funding source and even assist with due diligence. Another role for a good advisor is keeping things on track and helping iron out differences when problems or issues occur in the process—I like to think of a good advisor, as the level headed person in the middle that facilitates opposing forces as they come together for the collective benefit. Finally, a good advisor is usually a source of business experts who can assist the company, or assist in the transaction, such as attorneys, accountants, potential board members, and the like. Advisors who can provide these services may be BDs, or they may not be BDs. They may call themselves investment bankers, or they may not call themselves investment bankers. Thus, in looking for someone to help raise capital, it is important to understand exactly what services are being provided.

The mistake many CEOs make, particularly in companies that are already established, is that they don't think they need someone with these skills to help in the process. They give the old "Hey, my father founded this company thirty years ago, we hit three hundred million dollars a year in revenue last year, and we don't need anyone to tell us what to do or how to do it. Just get us in front of the money guys, and we'll sell them on the deal." Unfortunately, some of these CEOs need the most help. Their arrogance and know-it-all attitude wastes a lot of time and causes their staff and advisors a lot of aggravation.

The second task of an intermediary is that of a finder. A finder is a person who introduces the company to the funding source. There are many finders who will do none of the advisory work discussed previously. They will take whatever materials the company provides, in whatever shape they may be, and send that information to actual funding sources, or to other intermediaries, to get the money. Their methods differ—some work with a small group of funding sources and act as "scouts," some have a large database of money sources, and they hammer the phones; some hold conferences to which money guys are invited and at which the company presents its story.

The first question you need to answer is what you are

looking for in an intermediary. Do you want an advisor, or a finder, or both? In some cases, one person or firm could perform both roles, but in some cases, it could be two different people or firms. You may think you have your act together and don't need an advisor, just a finder. I recommend you have both, and if you don't have any money to pay an advisor, find one who will work for stock and/or deferred compensation. You will need a finder unless you have experience in raising capital, or unless you hire an employee with experience in raising capital. <u>Just don't be fooled—most accountants, controllers, and chief financial officers have extremely limited experience in raising capital, and very limited skills in what it takes to bring money in, regardless of what they say on their resumes</u>. But if you can find a CFO who also has expertise in raising capital, he/she will be worth every penny you have to pay.

The next question that comes up is how these intermediaries get paid. Well, first, you need to be very clear about exactly what services they intend to provide, and what promises or commitments they tend to keep. Intermediaries, whether a Wall Street investment banker, or the guy who works out of his garage, are notorious for what is called "best efforts contracts." These contracts allow the intermediary to represent the company in its fund-raising efforts. The intermediary tries to get some sort of upfront fee (which with a Wall Street firm could be hundreds of thousands of dollars), but the contract promises nothing in terms of actual performance. The commitment under the contract with the intermediary can be as simple as "assist the company in raising capital as an advisor on a best efforts basis." Now, what exactly does that mean? Whether you are working with an advisor, or a finder, or both, you want to have everything spelled out in detail of what you can expect in terms of performance.

If it's an advisor, you might have the following deliverables in the contract.

The advisor will:

- Assist the company in the preparation of a two-page marketing piece.
-     Review the company's strategy and business plan and recommend changes.
-     Review the company's financial projections.
- Assist the company in developing alternative financing plans.
-     Assist the company in preparation of a PowerPoint presentation.
- Review management's oral presentation and recommend changes.
- Introduce the company to broker-dealers who could undertake a public offering of the company's stock, and
-     Help the company find a new corporate attorney.

If it is a finder you are dealing with, the agreement might include:

- Spend a minimum of ten hours per week, making phone calls to private equity funds and venture capital funds on behalf of the company.
-     Arrange a week of meetings in New York to introduce the company to BDs and equity funds and attend those meetings.
-     Produce a weekly report of every person contacted, with the firm's name, phone number, and email, and the interest level of that party, and next steps, if any.

Anyway, you get the picture. You need to set up expectations, and monitor productivity, otherwise, you will go three or four months down the road and still not have your funding, which may leave you with the feeling that nothing has been done. And you may be right. There are intermediaries who charge up-front or monthly fees, and their goal is to get as many fees as they can, rather than delivering anything concrete to the clients. When the client gets pissed off and cancels the contract, they just go on to the next client.

Further, in addition to setting up expectations, you will need to manage your intermediary. Any Wall Street investment banker reading this is going to say this advice is for the company that hires the guy who works out of his living room. Wrong!! A close friend of mine is the number two guy at a company with revenues of about $50 million. The company is growing like wildfire. The company needed a major investment of capital, so management went to one of those big-name Wall Street firms. They signed an investment banking contract with a fee of half a million dollars—that's right $500,000. My friend tells me that he has spent the last six months telling that Wall Street firm what to do, whom to talk to, how to sell his deal, and needs to barrage them with phone calls and emails on a daily basis to keep them focused and on track. He thinks he'll get the money, but says he is completely worn out at trying to get these money guys to do what he is paying them a lot of money to do. The moral of the story? You need to manage anyone you hire to help you with the money-raising process. Set expectations, get reports, make suggestions, ask them if they have done this or done that, and don't just leave them to their own devices, or they may not be working on your deal.

In terms of paying intermediaries, several issues arise. Should you pay up-front or monthly fees? Or should you pay on some sort of success fee basis? Or both? That is a decision you must make based on the money you have now, what your expectations are, and how the intermediary operates. I can tell you some of the best money raisers only work with up-front or monthly fees, but if you cannot afford them, then it is a moot point. On the other hand, those who charge success fees may only be less than energetic in working your deal. They may introduce it to three or four money guys, but if they can't get a fast deal, it may sit on their desk while their attention goes off to another deal they are working on.

There are a couple of other things to watch out for. First, many intermediaries will get you to sign an "exclusive agreement." Be very wary of this type of agreement. The intermediaries will tell you they need exclusivity because they will add so much value to the process, and that even if they don't raise the money, it will help you raise it somewhere else. In such a case, you may want to carve out a fee for that service specifically, different from the actual fund-raising fee, solely to compensate them for that added value service. However, in my experience, very few intermediaries I have ever worked with have added that much value (I have, but that's another story!). If you spell out in writing (see example above) what they must do under the agreement, you may consider it. However, I would make them reduce their success fees on any money that you bring to the table through your own efforts and personal contacts. I was involved in one fundraising effort for $6 million that was written as an exclusive contract. The intermediary brought in $4 million of that raise. The management team, through personal contacts, brought in $2 million. The intermediary got paid 12 percent on the deal, which means the intermediary got $240,000 on the money raised by management, for which they did absolutely no work. I don't think that's fair.

The advantage of a non-exclusive agreement is that you can have more than one intermediary working on the deal. As mentioned, intermediaries will tell you that might lessen their focus. My experience is most intermediaries work their contact base. They have a few dozen to maybe fifty private equity funds, venture funds, banks, high net worth individuals, and non-bank lenders with whom they work. They take your deal to their database of contacts. If no one is interested, the deal goes on the shelf, and further work is done on a "back burner" basis, which means they will only mention your deal if they accidentally come across a new funding source that specifically is looking for your type of company. Now, each intermediary has his own network, so if you have more than one working, you can tap into more than one network.

This chapter would not be complete without mentioning the legality of paying success fees. Many intermediaries and companies enter into agreements whereby a success fee is payable if money is raised and many companies pay those success fees. The general interpretation of success fees is that under Securities and Exchange rules and regulations, registered broker-dealers (BDs) can charge success fees, and other consultants and advisors who are not BDs cannot charge success fees. All that being said, I know of many instances in which a company paid a success fee to an advisor or consultant who was not a BD. Further, certain state laws conflict with the SEC rules. In California, success fees are allowed for non-BDs if certain guidelines are followed. I had one attorney tell me that if a success fee is paid to a non-BD, the SEC could reverse the funding and force the company to give the money back to the investors. However, I asked the attorney to cite an instance where that had occurred, and he could not. In a transaction I was associated with a company paid a success fee to a non-BD, and the executives of the company were all attorneys, and the money came from a fund, and the fee was agreed to by the attorney who represented the fund. Clearly, this is a fuzzy area. BDs don't want non-BDs to charge success fees because BDs want to capture all of the business for themselves. On the flip side, BDs also want to focus on the most lucrative opportunities, so that means BDs will not take on many early stages and start-up fundraises. My advice is to seek counsel from your attorney if a non-BD consultant or advisor wants a success fee, and if your attorney is adamant about not paying a success fee, then tell the attorney to figure out how to compensate the advisor in a manner that does not require cash up-front.

A final word on intermediaries... Intermediaries get paid for their knowledge and their contacts. They understand how the capital raising process works, how to improve your chances of success, who the funding sources are, and how to contact those funding sources. And while it may look to you like all an intermediary did was make one phone call to raise your money, the fact is that it may have taken twenty years to build the relationship where that one successful phone call could be made. If an intermediary helps you raise capital, he deserves to be paid. I would say that even if you don't have an agreement in place with that intermediary, he still deserves to be paid. I know a lot of intermediaries, and everyone has a story about being screwed out of a fee by a prior client. That's just plain wrong. Do the right thing. If someone helps you get the money you need for your business, pay him/her. And if you are not comfortable paying what might be perceived as a success fee, hire the intermediary as a business advisor or consultant to assist in deploying the capital you have raised to grow the business.

IT'S A SECRET!

Previously, the subject of confidentiality agreements or non-disclosure agreements was mentioned. There is a third agreement that is often combined in a non-disclosure agreement, and that is a non-circumvent agreement, but let's talk about non-disclosure agreements first. These agreements are often referred to as NDAs.

If you ask your attorney, he/she is going to tell you that everyone you talk to about your business should be signing an NDA. Ideally, he/she would like to get involved with the signing of these agreements for your protection (nothing to do with fees, of course). However, the reality is that in most instances, an NDA is unnecessary, and in those instances where it is necessary, it provides limited recourse to the aggrieved party. Now, I am not saying you shouldn't get NDAs signed, but what I am saying is you need to use them with proper thought to avoid looking foolish. I've had guys in the bar, upon being asked about their business, whip out an NDA from inside their coat pocket and expect to collect a signature. If you can't tell someone about your business in a five to ten-minute conversation, without disclosing something that is so confidential and sensitive such that it risks your business, then you better go back and come up with a new pitch.

<u>Most money guys are money guys.</u> Money guys work for banks, lenders, investment funds, and the like. And while they

may think they could run your business better than you do, the last thing in the world they want to do is run your business. They would rather give you the money, have you do all of the hard work, show up every once in a while to let you know everything they think you are doing wrong, and never have to worry about making payroll, shipping product, or battling competitors for market share. The risk of them looking at your well-crafted business plan and deciding to quit their jobs and go into business is extremely unlikely. It's far more likely that if they really like your business, they'll give you the money.

<u>What is confidential?</u> Having read hundreds of business plans, seen hundreds of presentations, and heard hundreds of pitches; there is very little in most business plans that is really all that confidential to the degree that should a money guy choose to disclose the information, which he probably won't, it would do any harm. Coca Cola wouldn't put the formula for Coke in their business plan, and if you had a similar proprietary or patented process, you wouldn't include all the details in your business plan either (we've already discussed what to include and what not to include in your business plan). Let's say you are a competitor to Coke. After years of research, you've finally developed a secret formula for a new cola, and in blind taste tests, you win out over Coke every time. You won't include the formula in your business plan, but you might give the money guys a sample. What's the worst that can happen? The money guy mentions to one of his buddies that he met with someone who has a better-tasting cola to Coke. So what? The fact is that the overwhelming success factor in your business is your ability to execute on the plan. There are hundreds if not thousands of companies who thought they had something that tasted better than Coke, and all but a handful are no longer in business. Why? Because execution is as important, and generally more important than confidential know-how.

<u>The money guys deal with confidential information all the</u>

time. Money guys are used to confidential information. They learn all sorts of things from clients and potential clients, and they are just not in the habit of blabbing everything they learn to a whole lot of people. Much like a doctor or an attorney, money guys tend to keep information given to them between them and the people that gave them the information.

If you insist, you may lose out on a funding source. Some money guys just won't sign them. In some larger firms, they are prohibited from signing them (you can thank the attorneys for that). In some cases, they may want you to use their version (in which case you will want to check with your attorney, which will cost you money). If you are too pushy about NDAs, you will lose part of your potential audience.

OK, so now you ask, "Well, what about all the stuff in my due diligence package?" Remember, the information in the due diligence package is supplied after you have a term sheet. And if you review the chapter on term sheets, what is one of the components of a term sheet? A confidentiality clause. Now, with a signed term sheet in hand, you're protected at a time when you may be disclosing something that is really confidential.

At the beginning of the chapter, I mentioned something called a non-circumvention agreement. Non-circumvention agreements and/or non-circumvention clauses are typically used when one party doesn't want the other party to go around the first party. This can work in two ways. You may be approached by an intermediary who thinks he has a funding source for your deal. He doesn't want you talking directly to the funding source and trying to cut him out of the deal. It is very appropriate that he gets you to sign a non-circumvention agreement, and in fact, even without the non-circumvention agreement, it is really unethical for you to try to go around the intermediary if you don't already know the funding source in question.

A similar situation could occur if you have in your business plan the completion of a transaction that is contingent upon you raising capital. You may have lined up an acquisition, have an agreement to purchase a license or patent, or perhaps have an option on a piece of property. The last thing you want is someone who looks at your deal trying to go around you and trying to complete that transaction themselves, with the idea of trying to do what you planned to do, or even worse, earning a fee by flipping the transaction back to you. In such cases, you want to get a non-circumvention agreement signed, and if possible, even have stated in the non-circumvention agreement a specific fee that would be owed to you by the other party, if that party did go around you.

Again, if you are involved in any such situation, never go around anyone, even if you don't have a non-circumvention agreement in place. It's simply unethical.

THE NAME GAME

Previously, we mentioned advisory boards. It is a good idea to have an advisory board, particularly if you use it. However, money guys know that many advisory boards are just for show. It's great if you can get some known commodities (that means people with recognizable names or whose achievements in some field give them expert status) to sit on your advisory board, but don't dwell too much on their ability to open doors or get you business. In fact, if they can do any of that, get them to do it; then you can tell the money guys what happened, as opposed to what is going to happen.

Something that goes together with advisory boards is name-dropping in general. I once sat in a meeting up in the San Fernando Valley, just north of Los Angeles. The gentleman in front of us was supposedly in the music business, and he had come up with a new idea for distributing music. He was not looking for very much money, but of course predicting wildly optimistic financial results. When I questioned him on some of his logical premises, he went into a tirade about his knowledge of the industry. We happened to be facing south, and our view was the Santa Monica hills, upon which are perched mansions, many of which are owned by people in the music business. This gentleman points toward the hills and proceeds to tell us about how well connected he is in the industry. He rattled off the names of a half dozen super-performers like Madonna and Stevie Wonder, not to mention the CEOs and presidents of major record labels. He was a welcome guest in the homes of these people, had partied with them, attended weddings, and so on. I did a little mental calculation and figured that the group of folks he had name-dropped probably spent as much money as he was looking for on their weekend bar tabs, and if he were that well connected, he would certainly be able to hit some of these "good buddies" up for the money. Needless to say, my interest in assisting this individual in raising capital for his venture immediately disappeared.

The point here is that no one cares whom you know, what favors you think you can call in, and how connected you say you are. And the more time you spend bragging about how connected you are, the greater chance you have of being labeled a "slick salesman" or a "phony," as opposed to the competent CEO of a company. So, let me repeat. If you are well connected with influential or famous people, show how that has benefited you, not what you expect those connections to deliver in the future.

FINANCE 101

I hate to burden you with a discussion of finance and accounting. I know not every CEO can be an accountant or finance major. But there are a few basic concepts of accounting and finance that you need to understand. There are some very good quick guides to accounting and finance that you may want to buy, and when you have some time, read. If you are the CEO of a company of reasonable size, you need to be able to read financial statements, even if you came up through the ranks of sales or production. Money guys don't expect CEOs to necessarily be financial whizzes, but it will keep you from putting your foot in your mouth if you have a basic understanding of a few concepts that are important to lenders and investors. We'll talk about a few of the most important here.

Return on investment. Commonly called ROI, the return on investment is simply the money that the money source makes on your deal. It is often referred to in terms of a per annum percentage—such as the ROI is 30 percent. It seems simple enough, but you would be surprised at how some seemingly sophisticated people get this wrong. Let's look at an example.

An investor invests $100,000 in business at the beginning of year one. At the end of year three, the fledgling company is sold to a bigger company, and the investor gets back $220,000. So, over the course of three years, the investor made a gain of $120,000. That works out to $40,000 per year. $40,000 divided by $100,000 is 40 percent, so the ROI was 40 percent per annum. I have seen people who said the ROI was 210 percent. That is correct over the entire three-year period, but when we speak of investment, we typically speak of a per annum return, because that is how we speak of the cost of money when we talk about loans or other financial instruments.

Likewise, if an investment of $100,000 returns $110,000 in two months, the ROI is not 10 percent, it is 60 percent per annum ($10,000 for two months would equal $60,000 per year).

Understanding this return on investment number is important because it is what the money guys will look at in assessing the risk/reward ratio of your deal. It also helps you understand what to expect. If mortgages that are secured by real estate return 7 percent, then a risky start-up venture with no assets better gives the investor a substantially greater return than that, or you'll never raise the money.

Revenue, income, and profit. This topic also seems straightforward, but I have seen CEOs of large companies use these terms incorrectly. Revenue is the money you generate from the sale of your products or services and is interchangeable with sales. (Even though the government calls the money it collects in taxes "revenue," it really is not, because revenue occurs when there is a sale, and a tax is not a sale—but that's another story.) Profit is what is left over after you collect your revenue and have paid your bills (and if there is not enough revenue to cover your bills, then you have a loss). Income can have several different meanings. Sometimes people say income when they mean revenue. Sometimes people say income when they mean profits. Net income generally does mean profits. My advice is to stay away from the word income because there is some confusion about its meaning. If someone asks you a question about income, ask them to clarify—do they mean revenue or sales, or do they mean profits?

Cost of Goods Sold Vs. Contribution Margin. Someone may ask you, "What are your margins?" Years ago, the terms "margin" and "gross profit" were often used interchangeably. The typical calculation would be sales minus cost of goods sold. However, due to the proliferation of outsourced business services, many companies have shifted what used to be fixed costs to variable costs. Now gross profit is typically calculated at sales minus costs of goods sold, where gross margin is typically calculated as sales minus variable costs.

Let's say a company is selling a product for $50 over the Internet. The product costs $20, and the company pays a 3rd party fulfillment house for shipping, and that company charges $8 per until shipped, and the company markets everything on Amazon, and Amazon charges a 10% marketing fee. Gross profit is sales minus product cost, or $50 minus $20, which makes the gross profit $30. Gross margin is sales minus variable costs, or $50 minus product costs of $20, fulfillment cost of $8, and Amazon marketing fee of $10, which makes the gross margin $12.

Why is gross margin important? For two reasons. First, the gross margin tells a business how much of each sales dollar is available to cover fixed costs (fixed costs are those costs like rent, salaries, insurance, and so on that tend to stay constant from one period to the next). Second, if you know the company's fixed costs, you can quickly calculate breakeven. Breakeven is the point at which the company makes zero profit or loss. Breakeven plus one moves the company into profitable territory. So, using our example, let's say the company's fixed expenses were $120,000 per month. The company would need to sell 10,000 units per month to breakeven, or $500,000 in sales. Breakeven and gross margin are two very important concepts, and if you are raising money, you need to understand these concepts and know how to calculate them.

Security. Most businesspeople understand that lenders look for security to secure their debts. What some business people do not understand is that when a lender talks of security, he or she is talking about having an asset that he/she can seize and sell to someone else to pay off the debt, in case the debtor does not pay it off. The items that can be sold most readily, and at the most predictable prices, are real property, inventory, accounts receivable, and machinery. Goodwill, customer lists, trademarks, trade names, and other items may have a value, but the value is often very difficult to establish, and some of these items are impossible to sell.

Sometimes lenders will ask for a personal guarantee as security. Asking for a personal guarantee is very normal for early-stage companies, or in those instances where the company is not performing well financially or does not have the security within the business to support the loan. Also, lenders believe that if the CEO is willing to put up his or her personal assets, he/she has more faith in the ability of the business to succeed.

The point about security is to understand the way lenders and money guys think about security. Security is something that secures the debt; it is not a measure of the risk in the deal. Let me give you an example. I worked with a company that was in a very fast-growing industry, and this company was growing very rapidly, and becoming profitable. We were sitting in front of a traditional banker, and when the subject of security came up, the CEO kept alluding to the industry growth rates and history of profits as security. While that may provide some comfort to the bank, it is not what the bank considers security. Security is something that the lender can attach a legal claim to, often registered with the government, which allows them to grab the asset and sell it, should you not pay them back.

Burn Rate – Another term you are expected to know as the

CEO is your burn rate. Burn rate is the amount of cash, usually expressed on a monthly basis that the company is spending, over and above any cash inflows. Note that the burn rate does not necessarily equate to income statement loss. A company could be losing $10,000 a month on its income statement, but in addition, it could be investing $15,000 a month into software that is capitalized on the balance sheet. In this case, the burn rate would be $25,000 per month. If the company has $150,000 in cash in the bank, and if it continues to burn $25,000 per month, the business will run out of cash in six months.

Cash Flow and Cash Needs - CEOs are also expected to understand the cash flow and the cash needs of their business. Note that cash flow and profits are not the same things. A company can be profitable and still run out of cash. How is that possible? It is easy, and it happens all the time. Businesses often spend money on assets that do not appear on the income statement but rather appear on the balance sheet. Those items include such things as accounts receivable, inventory, equipment, intellectual property, and deposits. The investment in assets for many fast-growing companies far exceeds the internally generated profits from the business. Therefore it is important that you understand how much cash your business will need, what the business will use that cash for, and how much of that cash will be generated internally (from profits), from debt (through accounts payable, lease financing or other loans) and from equity.

THE DEAL KILLERS
AND THE YES MEN

There will come a time when you must decide to go through with a funding or not. Most CEOs will turn to their advisors to get some feedback. The problem with advisors is that they run into two categories—the deal killers and the yes men.

The deal killers are against the deal. There can be several reasons why. They may have a vested interest in keeping you as a client. The small-town accounting firm and law firm know that if you get that $25 million from Wall Street, the money guys are going to force you to use some big national firm. Accountants and attorneys are often conservative. They look at all the things that can go wrong, and very often are not adequately able to evaluate those downside risks against the upside. Also, if they greenlight the deal and it doesn't work, they worry you will come back to them and blame them for it. If they pooh-pooh the deal and it does work, well you'll probably forget their advice in your euphoria over success, and again, may not be using them anymore because your business will have graduated to the next level of accounting and law firms (who by the way, will do exactly the same thing, when you're ready to go to the next level again). The approach I suggest you take is to get your accountant and attorney together, and let them know that their job is to figure out a way to do the deal because you want to do it and that their jobs are to protect you from the downside risks as much as possible. Then ask them to focus on that aspect of the transaction; otherwise, they will be running around shouting danger with no idea how to solve it. Many times, in working with attorneys, in particular, I have told them that they could only point out something bad in a funding document if they have a reasonable and supportable suggestion for fixing it, and if they can quantify the risk. Otherwise, they'll waste thousands of dollars arguing with the money guy's attorney about whether or not the money guys have the right to put the loan into default should the country be attacked by green men from outer space.

As bad as the deal killers are the yes men. The yes men come in two forms. They are either people who have a vested interest in the deal being funded, or they are people whose career rests on the goodwill of the boss. People who could have a vested interest if the funding comes through include middlemen, brokers, advisors, and even senior employees. These people may get success fees, consulting fees, raises, or other financial benefits and they may be so exuberant about lining their pockets, that they really don't consider the deal, and any alternatives, from an unbiased perspective. The other yes men are ones whose livelihoods are at the whim of the CEO. Now, I've read all of those management books by Warren Bennis, Ken Blanchard, and Tom Peters, and we know a great CEO wants to be challenged by his employees, wants them to be open communicators, wants to make collective decisions, and wants to make informed decisions after listening to the input of others. OK...that's five CEOs in this country (one of those, my friend Kevin, is probably the best CEO on the planet, probably underpaid for what he does, and could write the book on being a great CEO—maybe he will). The rest of the CEOs want their management team to go along with whatever they say, and if any member of the management team crosses the boss, he or she is marked, and his/her career at the company is over.

What is the solution? First, if the CEO I have just described is you—change your ways. But assuming that may take some time, get an advisor, or group of advisors, who have the following qualifications: (1) have enough sophistication to really understand the deal and give appropriate advice, (2) have the time to look objectively at the deal, and (3) have no vested interest in whether the deal fails or succeeds. Then, once you have found these guys, use them, and listen to them. My recommendation is that every CEO needs at least one and maybe a couple of people like this—people who will be brutally honest, call a spade a spade, and who will be as tough on the CEO as the CEO is on his staff. And if you can't find someone who will do it for nothing, find someone who will do it for money—just make sure his or her compensation is not tied into the success or failure of your funding. By the way, I'd love to be that person. Helping CEOs see the light is one of my favorite past-times.

WHERE'S THE CROWD?

When I was helping companies raise money back in the 1990s, small companies could raise capital from small local and regional broker-dealers (BD). If you needed $1 million, you and your attorney put together a PPM (private placement memorandum), signed an agreement with one of the local BDs, and in a month or two, you would have your money. The BD would get a room full of salespeople who would call high net worth individuals like doctors, attorneys, professionals, and business owners and sell them on the deal, probably in increments of $10,000 to $20,000 per investor.

Could you engage one of those BDs today? Not likely. FINRA (Financial Industry Regulatory Authority) the body that regulates BDs (also called securities firms) reports that at the end of 2019, there were 3,517 BDs in the United States. In 2005, there were 5,102. That is a decrease of almost 30%. I recall reading an article some time ago (which I cannot locate) that back in 1990, there were more than 10,000 BDs. Why the drop? In part because increasing regulatory and compliance costs and the costs of insurance made small raises unprofitable for these local BDs. Simply put, a small BD could not cover costs of due diligence, insurance, commissions to its salespeople, and overhead on a small raise. I believe that part of the reduction in the number of BDs was orchestrated by the larger BDs that controlled the regulatory process to limit competition. The result was that BDs consolidated, many of them focused on larger dollar raises that generate more fees, and the access to capital for early-stage small enterprises dried up.

In any period of economic recovery, it is typical for small businesses to lead the way in generating new employment. Regulators and politicians recognized that as we were coming out of the 2008 recession, small businesses were not creating the jobs some experts believed they should be creating. Part of the reason was that the increased regulation on BDs and the reduction in the number of BDs restricted capital for new and early-stage enterprise formation. In response, on April 5, 2012, the Jumpstart Our Business Startups (The JOBS Act) was passed into law.

The JOBS act included several changes to the rules and regulations for raising capital for small, non-publicly traded enterprises, including changes to regulation D. Most important, the act contained new regulations under a section titled "Crowdfunding." Much of the fundraising for small non-public companies had been restricted to "accredited investors." Accredited investors are people who meet certain financial tests, such as income and net worth. Guess what? Most of us don't qualify! And probably most of the people you know don't qualify. Under the new crowdfunding rules, you could raise money from average Joes using comparatively simple documentation over what was previously required.

Great! The government provided a way for you to raise money from average people up to certain limits. It sounds simple – but it's not. First, even though the act was passed in 2012, the Securities and Exchange Commission did not publish the rules and regulations on crowdfunding until May 2016, four years after the bill passed. And when the rules did come out, they established that all crowdfunding must be done through "portals" and that the operation and regulation of these portals must be made through registered BDs – the very group that was in part responsible for the decrease in BDs that restricted access to capital for small companies in the first place. I think the phrase goes; this is like asking the fox to guard the henhouse.

So, is crowdfunding an option? Yes, it is, and there are two types of crowdfunding you can engage in. The first type is through platforms such as Kickstarter, Indiegogo, and Go-FundMe. In these platforms, you cannot sell what is considered "securities." That means you cannot sell stock, debt, or a combination thereof. You can, however, solicit donations, although the likelihood of getting donations for your company is very low. The best way to use these platforms is to sell some sort of promotional offers, such as a discount on future purchases, priority on the shipping of a new product, or some similar deal that is not available elsewhere. The good thing about these types of crowdfunding options is that the cost is very low, and you can get up and running very quickly.

The second crowdfunding options are platforms that allow for the sale of securities (as mentioned, that means stock, debt, or any combination thereof). But remember, you must go through a registered crowdfunding portal, and you still must comply with a host of SEC rules and regulations. Further, the portals typically charge both upfront fees to register, and fees on funds raised. You will also have to prepare certain information on the company, such as your business plan, management, details of your offering, and capital structure. You may also have to have financial statements prepared by an outside CPA firm (reviewed financials). Securities fund-raising sites include AngelList, SeedInvest, and EquityNet.

So how do you decide on whether you should move forward with crowdfunding? From my experience, whether you

are making a product offer based crowdfunding, or a securities crowdfunding, the most important indicator of success is
finding a crowd. The crowdfunding platforms are filled with
hundreds, if not thousands of opportunities, so it is unlikely
visitors to any given platform will find you and take the time
to review what you are offering. Those crowdfunding offerings
that work best are ones where the business already has a crowd
or can generate a crowd through some endorsement or marketing activity.

As an example, let's say you write a blog for people who
love horses, and you have 50,000 followers. Now you develop a
product that would be used by people who own horses. You already have a crowd – the 50,000 people who read your blog. You
can talk about your fundraising in your blog and direct your
readers to the fund-raising site.

Another example is a company that I know of that was
introducing a new brand of alcohol beverage. Now you would
think that the alcohol beverage market is mature, and raising
money for such a project would be tough. However, one of the
founders of the company knew a popular comedian who had
a significant following, and when that comedian endorsed the
product, the company was able to raise its target fundraising
goal in a very short period.

If you don't already have a crowd following you, or if you
have no quick way to build a crowd once you list your opportunity, then there is a very good likelihood that your crowdfunding will not be successful.

SEND ME AN ANGEL, RIGHT NOW

You may not remember the 80s song by Real Life, "Send Me Angel, Right Now," but I do, and every time I speak with businesspeople trying to raise money, it reminds me of this song. The singer appeals to heaven to send him an angel. It seems like I've heard lots of businesspeople also expecting an angel, hoping some miracle will get them funding as opposed to following the instructions in this book.

What is an angel investor? An angel investor is typically an individual who has had his or her own success, made a ton of money, and now invests some of that money, usually in start-up or early-stage companies. An angel may operate independently or may operate as part of a group. Today you will find many angel investor groups. In the Los Angeles area, there are the Pasadena Angels and the Tech Coast Angels. You can probably do a Google search in your area, check out meetup.com, or ask businesspeople you know, to find angel groups in your area.

Let's talk about individual angels first. If you can find one, great. But just because they are "angels" does not mean there is a commonality amongst them. I know an angel in his 80s who made his money in manufacturing and is not comfortable unless he can pick up a product and hold it in his hands. I know an angel in her 30s who made her money selling some tech company to Google and who doesn't understand anything but technology-driven opportunities. I have worked with a company in the telecommunications field whose angel acted like a bank – any time the company needed money, the angel wrote a check. Most angels I have met also want to give you more than just money – they want to be considered as advisors and help guide the entrepreneurial venture towards success. Some angels move quickly, and some do not. I obtained an investment from an angel for a client of mine. The angel agreed to the investment on a Wednesday, and by next Monday, the company had the money. To angels, much of the decision depends on their relationship with you and their trust in you delivering what you promise. Courting angels may be less about your business plan and projections and more about your personality and your vision. Finding individual angels is not easy. They don't advertise, and they typically only look at opportunities from their own circle of acquaintances and friends. Finding individual angels requires a lot of legwork – attending events, working your network, and following up on referrals.

Angel investor groups operate very differently from most individual angel investors. Angels join angel investor groups for several reasons. One reason is the camaraderie. Angels get to talk business and invest with other angels. Another reason is deal flow. An angel investor group is going to see many more opportunities than an individual angel might see, so there is a better opportunity for the angel to find the best deal. There is also the theory that two heads are better than one, so having another angel confirm what the first angel thinks about a deal, good or bad, is reassuring. Finally, angel investor groups have a lot of processes administered by the group members, including reviews, critiques, pitches, more pitches, and so on. All of this gives the angels something to do.

Working with angel groups is going to be much more formal than working with individual angels. Often you will have to submit your information through the angel group's website. An associate of mine with Pasadena Angels in Los Angeles says that 80% of the submissions are immediately rejected. Then, if you do get to the next phase, the angel group may want you to submit your information in its prescribed format. That's right. Even though you have all the nicely prepared business plans and PowerPoints, it is likely you will be requested to answer numerous questions in the format as laid out by the angel group. At the end of this chapter, you will find a sample angel group information request list.

Upon submission of the angel group information request, you will then be subject to the angel group's process, which differs from one angel group to the next. Some will want presentations, some will want meetings, and some will want answers to additional questions. You will need to work through the angel group process at the end of which the angel group may make you an investment offer. Do angel groups fund? Yes, they do. Are the chances very high? Probably not. Further, while this is not always the case, in some instances, angel group offers can be very one-sided – they demand a huge ownership interest in the company for a relatively small investment.

Something else to watch out for. Often working your deal through the angel investor group process is time-consuming. It can take many months. And even when the indications are promising, you might not get funded. I met an entrepreneur whose business plan was weak. I didn't think he had logically thought out how to penetrate his market, how to generate revenues, and how to grow the business. I suggested he engage me to assist in working through those issues. He insisted that his business had been well accepted by two different angel groups. Months went by with meetings, more meetings, phone calls, and so on, but at the end of the day (or more accurately after six months), both angel groups passed on his deal (they are angels, not fools).

Should you bother trying to work with angels, either individual angels or angel investor groups? The simple answer is "that depends." If you are an early-stage company with a few options, you need to explore every opportunity to raise capital. If nothing else, seeking out angel investors will get you networking, talking to people, and getting feedback on what potential investors think of your business. Even if you don't get the funding from the angels, you may improve your plan and your pitch, and that will help you get the money from some other source. Also, business is about networks and contacts, and knowing angels (AKA people with bucks) is never a bad thing.

Below is an example of what you could be asked to provide by an angel group. Obviously, it can take a long time to answer all these questions, but going through the process can help in vetting the business concept and in building an improved business plan and strategy.

1. Deal Summary document: a summary of the investment deal thesis

2. A financial model with 3-5 year forecast and all actual historical numbers for the company since its inception

3. Valuation: How much is being raised, and what is the pre-money and post-money valuation

4. Pre-round cap table: Cap table showing ownership prior to current raise/round.

5. Post-round cap table: Pro forma cap table showing ownership after current raise/round.

6. Prior round documents: Copies of all term sheets/ notes/contracts/documentation from prior rounds.

7. Current round documents: Copies of current term sheets, notes, and other documentation that will be utilized as a part of this round.

8. Specific questions, to be answered and signed by Entrepreneur:

    i. Are any loans to Founders or other entities being paid off via this funding?

    ii. Are any current salaries being increased because of this funding?

    iii. What are the option pool pre and post-funding (is the option pool being increased on a pre-money basis)?

    iv. If a convertible note: Can company prepay note without permission of note holder.

    v. Are there any current or foreseeable disputes over ownership of the company?

    vi. Are there any matters, which could reasonably be considered conflicts of interest on the part of the Founders and company management?

    vii. Are any of the Founders or key management team members currently employed outside of the company we are considering funding.

9. Use of Funds, broken down into basic high-level cat-

egories and corresponding dollar amounts.

10. A detailed budget for the next 12 months

11. Provide the company's most recent month-end bank statement

12. YTD and last two years year-ending financial statements:
    a. Balance sheet
    b. Income statement
    c. Statement of Cash Flows

13. Business Value Proposition
    a. What is the current market pain that the company is solving?
    b. Describe the company's solution [i.e., how is the company solving the pain described above?]
    c. How does the company make money (in words simple enough for a 5th grader to understand)?

14.   Competition - List the company's top 5 competitors, and for each, one short sentence for how the company differentiates from each

15. Company's sustainable competitive advantage [i.e., how will the company defend its profit margins in the face of future competitors, including those that try to copy your company's exact model/product?]
    a. Organizational Development - What is the company's:
    b. Vision
    c. Mission
    d. Operating principals (if any)

16. CEO's background

17. What are the company's critical success factors, and why is this team uniquely qualified to execute on this?

WHO'S WHO?

For businesses, there are lots of possible sources of money, but most likely, there are very few probable sources of money. Why? Because as we have discussed previously, most investors and lenders have their specific lending requirements, which may be dictated by policy, charter, or law. I often hear company executives throw around lender and investor terminology only to discover they really don't understand how the sources of funds are structured and what those sources actually do. Therefore, in this chapter, I am going to list possible funding sources and give you a description of what those funding sources are, and how they operate. This list probably does not include every funding source but includes most of the sources you will come across. Also, there may be some overlap in what funding sources will and will not fund, and in how they operate.

Commercial Banks – Commercial banks are the banks that everyone knows, such as Chase, Wells Fargo, US Bank, Comerica Bank, and Bank of America. These banks do lend to businesses. However, they typically look for a business that has security (remember our previous discussion on security) and a profitably track record. My experience is you will need three years of profits before getting a loan from one of these banks. The exception is if you have significant real estate holdings that you can put up as security, and of course, they would most likely expect the business owner to sign a personal guarantee.

Business Banks – Business banks are like commercial banks, but business banks tend to have mostly business customers with few consumer customers. Business banks compete with commercial banks, particularly for the very lucrative business sector called mid-market companies. A mid-market company is a company that needs enough financial services that will allow the bank to earn lots of fees. Business bankers tend to be more business savvy than typical commercial bankers and tend to develop personal relationships with their business customers. Business banks typically can customize their loan and financial services products to the business and like to develop long-term relationships with their customers. Much like commercial banks, they look to security and profits in making funding decisions. City National Bank, Citizens Business Bank, and American Business Bank are examples.

Merchant Banks - Merchant banks in the U.S. are financial institutions that deal with international finance for multinational corporations. Merchant banks traditionally perform international financing and underwriting, including real estate, trade finance, foreign investment, and other international transactions. They may be involved in issuing letters of credit and in the transfer of funds. They may also consult on trades and trading technology. Most likely, readers of this book will not need the services of a merchant bank.

Angel Investors – Angel investors are one of the primary sources of funding for startup and early-stage companies. Angels are typically high net worth individuals who have made money in their careers and now use some of that money to help fledgling entrepreneurs. Angels typically invest small amounts (less than $100,000) but have a high degree of discretion as to what types of businesses they invest in. A significant part of their decision is based upon their assessment of the character of the person they are funding. Often angels like to take an active role in advising the CEOs of companies in which they have invested.

Angel Groups – Angel groups are just groups of angel investors who typically work together to find investment opportunities. As discussed in the chapter on angel investors, these groups can be challenging to work with. However, if you get funding from an angel group, you have the potential to raise more money than from a single angel, as the angels pool their money in the angel groups.

Factors – A factor is a lender who buys your accounts receivable at a discount to its face value and then collects the funds from the customers. Factors typically charge high-interest rates, but for companies who have customers that take a long time to pay, this can be a good way to quickly get cashback in the business to finance more production. Factors come in all sizes. I know of a factor in Newport Beach, California, that uses his own money and only works with a small number of companies at a time. On the other side, there are some huge factors that operate nationwide. Factors are not so much concerned about profitability, but more about the quality of your customers and your terms and conditions of sale.

Purchase Order Financing – While factors finance accounts receivable, some lenders will also finance purchase orders. That means if you get a significant purchase order from a solid customer, the funding source will put up the capital needed not only for raw materials but also the labor to manufacture those raw materials into finished products. To get this type of financing, you will need to have a strong buyer for your product (such as Walmart, Costco, or some other big retailer), and you must have solid experience at being able to manufacture the products you want to sell. Interest rates will not be low.

Asset-Based Lenders – Asset-based lenders are lenders who look primarily to the value of the assets that you post as security as opposed to looking at profitability or cash flow of the business enterprise. While commercial and business banks do asset-based lending (they take assets as security), we typically think of asset-based lenders as private lenders who work on deals the commercial and business banks are hesitant to finance. Asset-based lenders will charge a higher interest rate than a bank in part to cover the added risk of lending to a company that may have significant assets but is not profitable. Asset-based lenders are good at financing businesses that have "big ticket" inventory items such as vehicles, RVs, construction equipment, boats, and aircraft.

Family Offices – A family office is a funding source typically run by a person or family that has made substantial amounts of money through some investment or by starting and selling a business. In years past, very high net worth individuals would have invested in a professionally managed investment fund or would have turned their money over to a wealth management firm. However, today many of these individuals like the idea of doing their own investing. The good thing about family offices is that they have a very high degree of discretion over what they can invest in (much like angel investors). Further, they can often move much more quickly than institutional funds (which we will cover later). I represented a client that received funding from a family office. The decision was made in the client's conference room on a Friday, and by the following Friday, documents were signed, and my client had the money. The bad thing about family offices is that they can be very hard to find and if you do find them very hard to contact. Many of them only look at deals brought to them by a select group of intermediaries (finders).

Venture Capital Funds – Venture capital (VC) funds are funds that invest in relatively early-stage companies with the hopes of picking the winners – those companies that will not only survive but will see tremendous increases in enterprise value. Years ago, VC funds might invest in startups. Today most VCs let early-stage companies get their startup capital from angels, crowdfunding, or family offices and wait until those businesses have reached a certain stage of development, revenues, or customer growth before investing. Most VC funds focus on some sectors (such as technology or consumer products) and tend to deploy larger amounts of capital into a fewer number of companies. VCs can spend a lot of time in the due diligence process (they do not move quickly), and many want representation on the company's board and may even want to influence or have a say in business activities. VCs also typically want a very large stake in the companies they finance, which means if you are the founder, your ownership interest could be diluted down to a small percentage of the company. However, if your company has the potential for explosive growth, it is very difficult to fund super high growth companies without getting financing from a VC.

Private Equity Funds- Private equity (PE) funds are like VCs in that the fund will make investments into several businesses. However, PE funds typically don't have the risk tolerance of VCs. A PE fund will typically invest in a company that is further along in its life cycle than a VC firm. PE firms will also fund leveraged buyouts. Each fund is different, but these funds will typically operate under some specific charter, which could include various business sectors, geographic regions, green energy, environmentally friendly, size of the investment, and so on. As an example, a PE fund purchased 50% of my client's company for $30 million. The PE firm brought in a new CFO, CEO, and COO to run the company. PE firms typically only invest in firms that have reached a certain milestone in revenues and profits, and often play the role of taking a successful company to the next level.

Hedge Funds – Historically, hedge funds were funds that "hedged" as a way of reducing risk. As an example, a fund might buy certain stock, while at the same time short-selling another stock. Some hedge funds probably still engage in those activities, but today we think of hedge funds as being funds that are more speculative than a PE fund, and nimbler than a VC fund. Hedge funds can move in and out of investments or loans quickly, and they entertain opportunities such as short-term investments, bridge financing, purchase order financing, and any reasonable proposal that can make an above-average return investment. I know of one hedge fund that will loan working capital to a business. The cost will be high, but the terms and conditions are much less restrictive than an asset-based lender or traditional bank. The idea is to finance the company while the company returns to economic health (which sometimes can occur very quickly) and then have the financing paid off by some other lending institution.

Insurance Companies – Insurance companies collect a stream of money over time (premiums on a life insurance policy) only to pay out a large lump sum in the future. The insurance company will invest the cash it has on hand, with the hope that before it must pay out the death benefit, the company can make a profit by putting that money to work. Obviously, an insurance company cannot be too risky in the investments it makes, and most insurance company funds are in such things as investments in blue chips stocks and large real estate plays. However, some insurance companies do allocate a small percentage of their portfolio to earlier stage investments. If you are looking for money for any sort of real estate development, insurance companies can be a good source.

Investment Bankers – There is a lot of confusion about investment bankers, and we talked about that a little bit on the chapter on intermediaries. Investopedia describes an investment banker as "an individual who often works as part of a financial institution and is primarily concerned with raising capital for corporations, governments, or other entities." The important thing to note is that investment bankers are, for the most part, intermediaries. They do not invest their own funds. They are paid a fee to help companies raise funds. Most investment bankers charge up-front fees for their services and an additional success fee if they raise you the money.

Corporate Incubators and Start-Up Funds – If you look at the world of innovation, you will find that often innovation is driven outside of the mainstream of big business. Why? If you go to business school, you will find theories suggesting that well-established companies are bureaucratic, not open to new ideas, lack innovation, myopic, not risk-takers, and a host of other reasons. Having worked for a few large businesses, I can tell you that it is true. However, many of the large businesses have a special division, group, or fund whose sole purpose is to seek out small entrepreneurial companies with new ideas and to invest in those companies. The upside is that these investors are typically more reasonable than VC investors are. The downside is that if your product or idea is good, you may be tied into these giants and may not have the opportunity to build your company independently.

Lending Platforms - A recent entry into the lending arena is lending platforms. Lendingtree.com is an example. Some of these platforms are peer to peer lending, and some are more like lead generators, whereby once you have entered your information, it is funneled to funding sources that have shown an interest in your type of business. These platforms apparently have raised considerable money for small businesses. I cannot speak to that because I have never known a company that has raised money from these sites. Nevertheless, I would not hesitate to check them out as part of your fund-raising research.

Leasing Companies – If your company requires equipment to operate, such as manufacturing equipment, trucks, forklifts, and other machinery, you may qualify to lease that equipment.

Leasing companies are not as concerned about profitability, and sometimes manufacturers have their own leasing programs as a method of facilitating the sale of their products. The underlying interest rates charged by leasing companies would be more than if you borrowed the money to purchase the equipment, but for early-stage companies and companies that are not profitable, you may not be able to borrow the money, so leasing might be a good alternative.

DON'T FORGET THE GOVERNMENT

When I went to business school, we were taught that a business could draw on three sources of capital – profits, the sale of equity, and the proceeds of debt. Today we must add another source: the government. It is an interesting dichotomy that while our governments (federal and state) have increasingly made it more difficult for businesses to raise capital, those same governments have created a plethora of programs and institutions designed to lend and even give money to businesses.

There are too many programs and departments to list in this book, but it is worth covering just a few. The federal government's primary vehicle of support for small businesses is the Small Business Administration (SBA). The mission of the Small Business Administration is "to maintain and strengthen the nation's economy by enabling the establishment and viability of small businesses and by assisting in the economic recovery of communities after disasters." SBA loans are made through banks, credit unions, and other lenders who collaborate with the SBA. The SBA provides a government-backed guarantee on part of the loan. Under the Recovery Act and the Small Business Jobs Act, SBA loans were enhanced to provide up to a 90 percent guarantee to strengthen access to capital for small businesses after the credit freeze in 2008.

SBA helps lead the federal government's efforts to deliver 23 percent of prime federal contracts to small businesses. Small business contracting programs include efforts to ensure that certain federal contracts reach woman-owned and service-disabled veteran-owned small businesses as well as businesses participating in programs such as 8(a) and HUB Zone. Another resource the SBA launched earlier this year (2020) is the SBA Franchise Directory, aimed to connect entrepreneurs to lines of credit and capital to grow a business.

SBA has at least one office in each U.S. state. In addition, the agency provides grants to support counseling partners, including approximately 900 Small Business Development Centers (often located at colleges and universities), 110 Women's Business Centers, and SCORE, a volunteer mentor corps of retired and experienced business leaders with approximately 350 chapters. These counseling services provide services to over 1 million entrepreneurs and small business owners annually. The SBA's budget is just shy of $1 billion, but even before the Covid-19 bailouts, the SBA had guaranteed some $42 billion in loans.

In addition to loans, the SBA also tries to help small companies find investors. If you go to the SBA website (www.sba.gov), you can download a list of institutional investors that includes contact names, email addresses, and phone numbers. However, before sending emails to any of these sources, or calling them, I recommend you try to find the investor's website. Most institutional investor websites will provide information on such things as the typical size of the investment, industry preferences, geographical preferences, stage of the companies they invest in, and so on. Many even include information on companies the investor has previously invested in.

Another federal program under the Department of the

Treasury is the Community Development Financial Institutions Fund (CDFI Fund), which plays an important role in generating economic growth and opportunity in some of our nation's most distressed communities. By offering tailored resources and innovative programs that invest federal dollars alongside private sector capital, the CDFI Fund serves mission-driven financial institutions that take a market-based approach to support poor communities. These mission-driven organizations are encouraged to apply for CDFI Certification and participate in CDFI Fund programs that inject new sources of capital into neighborhoods that lack access to financing.

In addition to those resources from the federal government, most states have a department or division that helps small businesses. Obviously, larger states with more money have more resources. As an example, in the state of California, there is the Governor's Office of Business and Economic Development (GO-Biz) that claims it "serves as the State of California's leader for job growth, economic development, and business assistance efforts." The website (business.ca.gov) says that it "offers no-cost consultation for incentive identification, site selection, regulatory or permitting compliance assistance, foreign direct investment, and export assistance." It is funny that the government has a department to help businesses wade through the swamp of regulations that the government itself created. How about creating a department to eliminate useless government regulations?

The website lists the following GO-Biz programs: Cannabis Equity Grants for Local Jurisdictions, Cal Gold, California Community Reinvestment Grants, California Competes Tax Credit, California Film Commission, California Made, I Bank, and International Trade & Investment. Again, it is beyond the scope of this book to explain all of these programs, but the point is they exist, and through these programs, the state government is loaning money, guaranteeing loans, providing tax credits, and providing outright grants to businesses. I attended a financial conference recently, and the keynote speaker was from the State of California. He said the state has 90 different departments and programs designed to help small businesses.

Today whether you are trying to raise capital or are just operating your business, you should research and become knowledgeable on how you can get assistance from federal, state, and local governments to help your business.

An additional recommendation is to also get to know your state and federal representatives. Some politicians try to do their jobs, and that means helping businesses that operate in their districts. Sometimes these politicians can influence grants that are made by the state and federal government to businesses. Both federal and state governments have a history of providing loans, grants, guarantees, and tax breaks to businesses that are in industries the government favors. As an example, a green energy company called Solyndra received a $535 million U.S. Department of Energy loan guarantee. Additionally, Solyndra received a $25.1 million tax break from California's Alternative Energy and Advanced Transportation Financing Authority. Both investors and senior advisors to Solyndra had very clear and strong political connections with politicians in the White House and Congress. You may not have that much influence, but you never know when knowing your local congressional representative might get you some free money.

BE AN ARTIST

I have mentioned many times that raising money is not easy. Sometimes no matter how hard you try, you will not be able to get investors to put money into your business. If that happens to you, something to consider is looking at some non-traditional ways of getting your business off the ground. Let me give you a few examples.

I worked with a company that was trying to introduce an alcohol beverage product. To maximize per unit profit, the CEO wanted to do a very large production run to bring his costs as low as possible. In developing his product, he had a custom bottle designed, which had to be imported from Taiwan and a special bottle cap that had to be imported from Italy. He wanted to use a prestigious formulation company for mixing the ingredients and a huge bottling company to bottle the product. The result was that he needed to raise about $1 million to launch the product. The initial production run needed to be about 150,000 units. He had offers from a local bottling company to use a standard bottle and a locally produced cap, which would reduce the first production run to 10,000 units. His margins would have been much smaller on a per unit basis, but at least he could have gotten into production, and if the product sold well, then change to the custom bottle. He would have none of it, and so as far as I know, never got his business funded or his product onto the shelf. If you're in the same position, think about how you might do a small test run even if you don't make any money, to at least prove there is a market for your product. Then, once you have some sales, raising money will be easier.

A company that I worked with manufactured a special use industrial product. The company really needed money to ramp up sales. The management team exhibited at an industrial trade show and was approached by a company doing business in Asia that wanted to purchase the product. Management made a deal with that company. They sold the exclusive rights to several Asian countries to that company for $1 million. That $1 million got them up and running. Consider if licensing your product or selling territories for your product might be a way to raise capital.

Another company I worked with manufactured a healthy beverage using fruit imported from another country. The company was really undercapitalized, and when sales began to increase, that capital squeeze only got worse. The CEO spent a lot of time looking for money but didn't have much success. Finally, he approached the company from which he was buying the fruit. After some negotiations, he was able to convince his fruit supplier to put working capital into the company and to provide extended credit terms in exchange for an equity stake in the company.

One more example. A client of mine developed a software product to be used by building owners and managers. The company had very limited product distribution. It needed to raise money to hire a sales and marketing team to get the product into the market. However, raising money for this type of company was extremely difficult. Finally, the company partnered with a national firm that served the same customer base, and for a little equity, that firm became my client's sales and marketing department.

The point of this chapter is to think about why you need to raise money. What are you going to do with that money? Is there any way that you could give an equity stake in your company to another company that could provide what you need? Could you license your product to someone else? Could you sell the rights for certain territories to someone else? Could you get extended credit from your suppliers? Could you form a joint venture with another company? There are many options available for getting resources to execute on the business plan that can give you the same or similar results to raising money.

ODDS AND SODS

In this chapter, I am going to cover a few miscellaneous other things to think about when raising money for your company. They are random thoughts with no particular order of importance.

Follow up. We talked previously about getting the information from everyone at a presentation and following up with a thank-you email. This same follow up mentality applies to everyone you meet in your capital raising activities. Keep the contact information of everyone you speak to, record the results of each conversation, and follow up again if you don't get a specific response from someone. Money guys are busy. They may say that they'll get back to you, but they may not, for a number of reasons. They may not want to tell you that they can't give you the money, they may be rude, or they may just be busy. It doesn't really matter. Pester them until you get a yes, a no, or "I can't do it, but try Charley at the bank across the street." Also, keep those contacts' information, because if they can't help you now, they may be able to in the future. Maybe your local bank won't give you a credit line, but after you raise $2 million in equity, the bankers might change their minds. Stay in touch with your money sources—it will pay off for you in the long run.

Education. Every time you are in front of a money guy, it is an opportunity for you to learn something. Let's say you get in front of a money guy, and he listens to your pitch over lunch. He probably won't say if he is really interested or not. He'll probably say that he'll get back to you or may ask you to send additional information. Maybe the discussion of your deal lasts forty minutes. Lunch is going to last another half hour. What do most CEOs do? They continue trying to sell their deal. It won't work. If the money guy is sold, he's sold. If he isn't sold, barraging him with another half-hour about your business is not going to sell him. I suggest you look at these situations as learning opportunities. Now is your time to learn something from the money guy. Ask him what he thinks of your business and if he has any ideas or suggestions. Ask him what type of an investor or lender would do your deal. Ask him what's happening in the financial markets. And when you ask these questions, take notes, and don't try to defend what you have done. The five minutes you waste trying to explain why you chose Seattle instead of San Francisco for your west coast office is five minutes when you might have learned something of value to help your business. Here's an example of one I've seen many, many times.

CEO: "So, what do you think of our business?

MG: "Very interesting. Don't you think you're going international a little too soon, though?"

CEO: "Not at all. Let me explain. You see, my cousin works with the state department, and he has this report on globalization, and we read Freidman's book...." WRONG!

Remember, you have already given your presentation and answered questions, and you asked the money guy for some opinions. This is the correct way to answer.

CEO: "Hmmm. Why do you think that?"

MG: "The medical industry operates quite differently outside the U.S. Your costs of operations could be a lot higher than you think."

CEO (scribbling furiously): "Good point. We'll have to take another look at that. Any other thoughts?"

Remember, the money guys may be arrogant, they may be busy, or preoccupied, or biased in their decision making, but for the most part, they are not stupid, and they generally have incredible knowledge about money, lending, investing, other industries, and even other countries. Get every piece of information from them that you can. Better to collect ten ideas and have nine duds and one gem, than to not collect any ideas at all.

WHERE'S THE
MONEY?

Okay, you've read every page so far and followed every word. You have a business plan, a two-pager, and a presentation. You've got your due diligence material together, you know how to act in meetings, you're ready to learn, you're not going to argue with the money guys, you know the process, and now all you need to do is find the money. What now?

Now you must begin looking for money sources, and there really are only two basic ways of doing this. You can do it yourself (or if in a larger company, have the CFO, or others in the management team help) or hire an intermediary. We've already talked about intermediaries, but much of what I am going to cover here applies if you do hire an intermediary because you can't leave it to the intermediary to do all of the work (see my story about my friend who hired the big Wall Street firm in the chapter on intermediaries). You still need to manage and be in control of the process. In fact, I think intermediaries can be even more effective if you do help them along.

The first thing you need to do is to find funding sources, and then you can use all of the tools you have learned in these books to try to get them to fund your deal. Finding funding sources is work. The good news is that it's not difficult to work. As you start to talk to people, you'll quickly figure out what type of funding source is going to be most suitable for your deal. Then you can do research to find more of the money sources that have the profile that you and your intermediary, if you are using one, can contact. Here are some guidelines for the hunt for money sources.

Talk to everyone. If you're trying to raise money, you want to cast a broad net. That means you need to talk to all those people who are in your personal network. That may include accountants and attorneys, fellow Rotary members, people at the country club, and members of your church. You never know where you are going to bump into someone that is a money source, or that knows a money source. Just one word of caution —don't be too aggressive. If you come across like a boiler room salesman, you probably won't get too many people interested, and further, you won't get the thing that is just as valuable - referrals. Sometimes the "this isn't for you" approach works well. It goes something like this.

George: "Hey, Bob. What are you up to? I haven't seen you at the club in a while."

Bob: "George, good to see you. Well, I've been busy. I'm trying to expand my business. Any chance I could tell you about it?"

George, looking at his watch: "Sure. Can you make it quick? I've only got a couple of minutes."

Bob: "Okay. This is probably something you're not interested in, but maybe you can point me in the right direction. I'm looking for five hundred thousand dollars to launch a new product. I think we can sell five million units to Wal-Mart year one, and probably get an ROI of about thirty percent to the investors. Let me email a quick summary, and maybe you can think of someone who might be interested. Oh, and next time when you have a few more minutes, the drinks are on me."

By approaching the money source this way, indirectly, you aren't coming across as asking him to invest directly; you are asking for his advice and assistance as a man in the know. Remember back to our chapter on presentations and questions. I'm the Man is all around, and I'm the Man loves to talk about himself and his great connections. But if you ask I'm the Man for the money directly, he may be put off because he's probably always being asked for money. But if you ask him to refer you to someone he knows, he can now impress you with his stories about the deals he's done and the people he knows, many of which may be valuable to you. And of course, to introduce you to others, he'll most likely look at the opportunity himself; and who knows, he might even put up the bucks.

Part of your task in talking to everyone is asking everyone you talk to for a referral to someone else you can talk to. Remember, the money guys all know each other, and they often trade opportunities back and forth, depending upon the deal flow and the type of deal.

<u>Find out whose funding your type of deals.</u> Today, with a computer and an Internet connection, you can do work that ten years ago would have been almost impossible. Lookup public companies in your industry and read their public filings. Those documents will tell you who is funding those types of companies. Then approach those funding sources with your deal.

Look into joining or attending meetings of financial people and funding sources in your area, or if budget permits, in financial centers such as New York. Many of these events are listed on the Internet, and for a fee, you can attend and schmooze with the money guys and find out who is doing what type of deals.

You can get lists of banks, investment bankers, funds, venture capitalists, and non-bank lenders off the Internet. Many of these lists also contain information about the types of funding these organizations do, and further, once you have the funding source's name, you can look up its website, and usually, it will say on the website what kinds of deals the funding source does. All you need to do is go into the search engine on your browser and type in such phrases as an angel investor, venture capital, business loans, leasing, or investment banker. You could spend days tracking down and pursuing these funding sources, and you may spend a lot longer than that. Just remember, you're competing with every other business out there that is looking for capital, so don't waste your time, or the time of these funding sources, until you are ready to do the best job possible of presenting your business to the money guys.

Present at or attend conferences. Presenting at conferences is something that costs money, so if you don't have the budget for it, then it's not for you. But it can be a very successful way to find capital. First, many of these conferences are attended by hundreds of money guys. Second, if you follow the rules in this book, you and your deal will look a lot better than most of the deals they see, so there is a good likelihood you'll get some interest. If you cannot afford to present at a conference, consider being an attendee at the conference. At these conferences, there are always plenty of opportunities to rub elbows with money guys during the presentations, at lunches and dinners, at special functions, and of course in the bar. Don't be too pushy but collect business cards, and then after the show calls the people you met and give them your pitch.

Hire an intermediary. We've talked about intermediaries in other chapters. The fact is, you will increase your success in raising capital with an intermediary, and the more you can spend, the greater your chances. Whether he/she is a finder or a consultant, a Wall Street investment banker, or a barfly with connections, your chance of raising capital goes up with someone outside working as part of your team.

Leave no stone unturned. There is no rule of thumb as to how many money guys you must talk to in order to get your money. It all depends on the deal, and some deals are just tougher than others. I have done deals where the money was raised with a dozen phone calls. And I remember one deal I worked on where I personally phoned over five hundred funding sources. The key is to keep talking to people, keep coming up with new funding sources to approach, and all the while continually improve your business plan, your presentation, and your pitch. Finally, if it is taking a while to get your funding, it doesn't hurt to circle back with people you haven't talked to in a while. Funding sources do change their funding parameters from time to time; sometimes they are busy, sometimes they are slow, and timing is important. If now is not a good time for a funding source because they are in the middle of closing three deals, keep them in mind for a repeat contact in a couple of months.

Networking. Some of the activities listed above involve networking; however, networking is so important that I have put it in this chapter under its own heading. One of the best skills you can learn as a businessperson is networking, and one of the best skills you can learn in fundraising is networking. If you are already a networking guru, great. If you're not, then you need to spend time honing your networking skills. Here are just a few suggestions for effective networking:

- If attending events, don't arrive late
- Smile a lot
- Don't take rejection personally, it happens
- If you're at an event, keep the alcohol-consumption low
- Don't run around with sticky appetizers in your fingers
- Be genuinely interested in other people

- Rather than pitching your deal, find out how you can help others
- Ask lots of questions
- Follow up with the people you meet.

There are many good books on networking, and if you have not read one, I encourage you to do so. Check out the classic by *Susan Roane: How to Work a Room.* I read it years ago, and it is still a great guide to developing relationships that are needed to find the people who will provide the money for your business.

TAKE THE MONEY!

I saved this chapter for the end because I think it contains one of the most important messages in this book. Previously we talked about getting a term sheet, due diligence, and the progression toward final documents and funding. However, a lot of fundings get hung up at the term sheet stage because of a reluctance to accept the funding structure that is being offered. We talked a little about being reasonable with respect to the valuation you put on your company or the cost of capital, but even when valuations and the cost of capital are reasonable, many executives get cold feet. There is always the worry in the backs of their minds that somehow another funding source is going to come along with a better deal, but if they have already accepted one deal, it may be too late to take advantage of a better offer.

How you respond to a term sheet depends a lot upon your situation. If you are looking for funding for some planned expansion, you have solid cash flow, and the timing of your expansion is not critical, then maybe you can take a "let's see what else is out there" attitude. Likewise, if you happen to be that lucky company that has a line-up of funding sources waiting to do the deal, it's a nice position to be in; use it to your full advantage if you can. I can recall raising capital for real estate deals back around 1980. The banks were literally standing in line to lend against a transaction—all of it on a non-recourse basis!

But those times in history are rare. The facts are that most companies don't have the luxury of having a line-up of funding sources, nor do they have the luxury of waiting until the financing source comes along. Most companies need cash and need it now, and even if the company is not cash strapped, there can be significant opportunity costs in waiting for the best funding deal. Competitive markets mean that if you are standing still waiting for money, your competitors are gaining market advantage on you, or the market is changing, and the bright idea you had maybe passé by the time you raise the capital and bring it to market.

So, what should you do? Take the money!! Now I have heard all the arguments—the interest rate is too high, they want too much security, we can't live with the restrictive covenants, and on and on. First and foremost, you want to do everything you can to get the best terms you can. Even if you have signed a term sheet, you can still renegotiate the small print as time goes by. But even if the terms aren't as good as you like, it is often better to go ahead with funding than to sit idly by waiting for something better, particularly if the need is urgent.

Of course, this is where you must do some real soul searching. Are your business prospects as good as you think they are? Can you turn the company around? Can you expand into new markets? Can you launch that new business? If you can, and you can make money at it, then typically, the cost of capital becomes a moot point. If you can't, then it's a moot point anyway.

If your business is wildly successful (like most CEOs think their business is going to be), then you can always pay off expensive debt and refinance with cheaper debt, or buy back stock in your company to increase your holdings, or get the board to give you a bonus for performance. But if you don't take the money, you won't be able to do any of these things because you won't be able to execute; and if you don't execute, what's the point?

This may sound simplistic, but I have lost count of the number of times I have urged a company to take financing, only to have the CEO reject it because it was too costly or he didn't like the terms. And in many of those situations, the company's fortunes worsened; and when they finally got money, it was at a much higher cost than the original deal. Or alternatively, they spent another six months looking for funding, lost time in moving their business forward, only to obtain funding down the road on terms no better than the ones they had rejected. Or worse, discovered that while they were busy trying to get better terms, some other company had already begun to penetrate their market with a similar, or even better, product offering.

Of all the decisions a CEO must make, I think the decision to accept funding is perhaps one of the most difficult. It is difficult because to accept funding, you take on an obligation of performance, and if you don't perform, it can be extremely costly. So, my advice is tailored as follows: Take the money, but double-check your plan and your confidence in executing on that plan. Then make sure you perform.

I had a client in the Midwest that paid off several bank credit lines with a non-bank lender. The lender advanced the company $16 million. I was hesitant for the CEO to take the money, as this lender was very different from the prior lenders. The other lenders were small-town bankers, and while the interest rates were reasonably high, there was little oversight of the company's operations. This non-bank lender, on the other hand, had a lending agreement with pages and pages of covenants and conditions, and complex formulas for advances and security. Each time the company broke any of the covenants or terms, it was subject to penalty charges. The CEO of this company was a risk-taker and a gunslinger and had built an empire through forty years of numerous business enterprises, doing about $100 million in revenue. But he was not buttoned-down and did not put a lot of resources into financial controls. Shortly after closing on the funding, he went into default, and with penalties and interest escalations, he ended up paying the lender approximately $8 million in interest and other charges on a $16 million loan. Yes, that's right—50 percent effective interest rate. At the end of the day, to get out from under this financing, he had to sell his "cash cow" business to pay off the lender, leaving the company with its marginal operations. The company subsequently had to file for Chapter 11 bankruptcy.

Yes, take the money—but then make sure your focus, every minute of every hour, is on making sure your business is successful. Of course, you will say, "Why else would I be in business?" I have asked CEOs the same thing. Why are you in business? (But then, that's another story and probably another book.) The point is, if you're confident you can execute, if you've checked all of the numbers, if you've done your market research, if you looked at your organization and the competition, and you are still confident you can do it, take the money. Money is hard to get, and when the offer is there, move on it. And show the money guys how you can take their money, and make money, and the next time around, you'll probably have a much easier time of getting it, and you'll get it at a much lower cost.

SUMMARY

When raising capital, you want to use any and every tool you can to make the process easier and faster. I hope the tools and information I have outlined in this book help you. I have included some summary information and reference material throughout the book to assist you further, including a step-by-step summary of the capital-raising process. Have a look at this information and use these summaries as checklists as you prepare the information you need, and as you go through the process.

As you put the information in this book to work, remember a few things. First, this book represents some of the wisdom I have gained in over thirty years of helping companies raise capital and in working with CEOs and funding sources, so understand that it contains information from the trenches —from personal experiences I have had and witnessed through those years. Second, it is a guideline; you still need to be flexible in dealing with funding sources. The way any given money guy operates may be different from what I have outlined, so be ready to modify and massage your application of my principles as needed.

If you take anything away from this book, remember the one most important message. Just as businesses compete with other businesses for customers, you and your business must compete against other businesses for capital. Your business will never be judged by the money guys based solely on its merits. It will always be judged in reference to other opportunities the money guy has to deploy his capital and the general trends in the marketplace. That only means it is extremely important you do everything you possibly can to make your company look the very best, and hopefully better than other opportunities, for the money guys who are going to look at you and your plan in all the ways we have discussed in this book.

One final matter. I consider this book to be a work in progress. I continue to learn new things that help me help companies raise capital. If you find something in this book useful, I would really like to hear about it. If you have another idea or experience that you think might be valuable, let me know, and maybe I can include it in the next edition. If you have used any of my techniques and it helped you get the capital you need, let me know too. If you've got a story to tell, tell it to me. I'd love to learn about your success and your failures, and any ideas you have that might help future readers.

If you think you might need some additional assistance in your search for capital, visit my website www.bizrap.org. My website is a resource for people looking to raise capital, and a resource for people with capital looking for opportunities. You will find additional information on the site that may be valuable in helping you properly package and present your company, more tips on raising capital, and access to people who may be able to help you with your fundraising activities. In fact, if you have a project you are working on and you need some help, don't hesitate to contact me. I'm always looking for the next opportunity.

Thank you for taking the time to read this book, and good luck to you in finding the capital you need. And, I hope you not only find the money you need, but that you are able to build the business of your dreams. Remember, your business doesn't have to be big or glamorous to be very rewarding.

Michael Manahan

mike@bizrap.org

ACKNOWLEDGEMENT

I wish to thank two good friends, Rana Thomas and Charles Yesson, for taking the time to read through my manuscript and for giving me ideas and suggestions. Unfortunately, my good friend Charles passed away a few years after the first edition of Secrets to Raising Capital was published. I would also like to thank the countless CEOs and senior executives that I have worked with during my career who have helped me gain the experience and knowledge to write this book.

ABOUT THE AUTHOR

Michael S. Manahan

Mr. Manahan is a financial strategist, change expert and educator. During his successful career as a financial executive and consultant, Mr. Manahan has helped companies raise in excess of $250 million. Mr. Manahan has worked with more than 100 management teams, as an external consultant or advisor, and as a member of  the management team. He has held the position of chief financial officer for four companies, including three publicly traded companies and a division of a multi-billion-dollar furniture manufacturer. He has held senior finance positions in several other companies.

Mr. Manahan has more than 30 years of financial, executive, organizational and strategic management experience with a diverse group of companies operating in such sectors as real estate development, industrial distribution, consumer and industrial services, computer software, Internet services, healthcare, food manufacturing, entertainment, energy, furniture manufacturing, Internet retailing, construction and consumer products. Further, Mr. Manahan has assisted companies in structuring and completing joint ventures, acquisitions, divestitures, financings and reorganizations, as well as coaching companies through the pre-IPO stage.

Mr. Manahan has extensive experience in SEC reporting, corporate finance, public markets, investor relations and corporate development. Pursuing a life-long love of educating, Mr. Manahan has held numerous engagements to coach CEOs the effective communication styles and management strategies, and is also a professor in the School of Business and Public Policy at California State University, Dominguez Hills where he teaches accounting and finance to CEOs of the future.

Mr. Manahan is a graduate of the British Columbia Institute of Technology with a major in financial management. In 2005, Mr. Manahan enrolled at Pepperdine University in the doctorate of the organization change program and completed the course work, although he did not complete his doctoral dissertation. Mr. Manahan received his Master of Business Administration from Pepperdine in 1992. Mr. Manahan lives in Long Beach, California and has two wonderful daughters, Genevieve and Kimberly.

BOOKS BY THIS AUTHOR

The Key To Landing A Job - The Interview

Hiring decisions are primarily based on the interview. Yes, you need a good resume, education, and job experience but what happens during the interview determines whether or not you get the job offer. A good interview can often outweigh a weak resume and experience. Yet most job seekers have very poor interview skills. Even professionals and highly educated candidates perform poorly in interviews. The good news is that you can learn how to excel during interviews. The Key to Landing a Job – The Interview is your source for all the techniques and strategies you need to ace the interview and get the job you want.

Made in the USA
Monee, IL
07 April 2021

65002286R00134